Fidelity without Fu

Fidelity without Fundamentalism
A dialogue with tradition

Gerard J. Hughes SJ

Paulist Press
New York/Mahwah, N.J.

First published in 2010 by
Darton, Longman and Todd Ltd
1 Spencer Court
140 – 142 Wandsworth High Street
London SW18 4JJ

ISBN 978-0-8091-4724-3

Library of Congress Control Number 2010932898

North American edition published in 2010 by
Paulist Press, Inc.
997 Macarthur Boulevard
Mahwah, NJ 07430
www.paulistpress.com

Phototypeset by Kerrypress Ltd, Luton, Bedfordshire
Printed and bound in Great Britain by Thomson Litho, East Kilbride, Scotland

Acknowledgements

Many friends and colleagues have encouraged me to write a book which would address the kinds of issue with which ordinary intelligent Christians are confronted when they try to think about their beliefs. I would like to thank them for their enthusiasm for the project, and for the many comments they have made as I endeavoured to carry it through. In particular, I would like to thank Maria and Peter Cockerill, Peter Edmonds, Fiona Ellis, Philip Endean, Paul Hamill, Deirdre Johnson, Nicholas King, Lucy Matheson, Bill and Monica Tomkiss, and Dagmar Winter, who in their different ways and from their various points of view have tried to enlighten me on everything from the Acts of the Apostles to Zulu proverbs. I hope I have responded to most of their criticisms, and gone some way to meeting the needs which they helped me to identify. I am most grateful to them all.

I would also like to thank the team at Darton, Longman and Todd, especially Brendan Walsh and Helen Porter, for the very generous help they have given me at every stage. I am most grateful.

Contents

Fundamentalism: A Preliminary Look   1

1   Tradition and Translation   6

2   The Pitfalls of Translation   10
A faithful translation? Some illustrative examples   10
Reaching across culture gaps   19
     How can we understand the ancients?   19
     Can we ever 'reach' others?   20
The perils of extremism   21
     How one gets in touch: the professional translator   21
     In touch with what? Postmodern scepticism   22
     It's really very simple: the rigorist   24
What makes cultural exchange possible?   26
The project again.   29

3   Beyond Mere Words   31
'Speech acts': what we can do with words   31
     Speech acts in general   31
     Three sayings of Jesus: how to take them?   33
Large-scale misunderstandings   37
     The infancy narratives   39
     The resurrection narratives   49

4   The Challenge of the Sciences   58
The birth of modern fundamentalism   58
Physics, astrophysics and Galileo   60
The age of the sciences: fundamentalist panic   67

5   Shifts in Philosophical Vocabulary   75
Was Jesus of Nazareth a human person?   75
What exactly is transubstantiation?   87

6   Behaviour in Different Cultures   98
How do we know what someone is doing?   98
   The fuzziness of action words   99
   The moral complexity of actions   100
   Fundamentalism and 'relativism'   104
      Moral relativism and moral absolutism   104
      Moral pluralism   109
What do we mean by the imitation of Christ?   112

7   Fidelity to a Moral Tradition:
   Living as They Lived?   118
Some (comparatively) uncontroversial examples   118
   Closeness to sinners and the outcast   119
   Collaboration and revolution   121
   Relations between churches   123
Some less simple examples   127
   Pacifism   127
   The priestly ordination of women   133
What if there is no tradition?   142
   Genetic manipulation   143
   Death and life   146
Coping with uncertainty   151

To Sum Up   155

Index   159

Fundamentalism: A Preliminary Look

Few people, even among those who would commonly be described as fundamentalists, would welcome being called one. It is not usually intended as a compliment, even though the precise criticism implied is often only vaguely hinted at. Sometimes the suggestion is that to be a fundamentalist is to be some kind of political extremist, with a tendency towards violence justified by an appeal to religion. People can speak of Islamic fundamentalists, Hindu fundamentalists, sometimes also of Buddhist and Tamil fundamentalists, where the common element is a political and cultural intolerance issuing in violence; a Roman Catholic fundamentalist recently assassinated a doctor who ran an abortion clinic in the United States. Exactly what the link is between such people's conduct and their religious beliefs is often very vague, and is in any case repudiated by their co-religionists, who are every bit as religiously committed as fundamentalists but who totally reject the implication that their religion justifies such actions. But there are also believers in all the major religions who, in a less violent sense, are accused of being fundamentalists because they adopt very literalist readings of sacred texts, or, on religious grounds, take up indefensibly conservative positions on morality or liturgy.

Yet there are – or at any rate there were – also people who are proud to be described as 'fundamentalists'. The term was first used by a group of Christian theologians in the early 1920s. In so describing themselves, they proudly proclaimed their desire to return to and protect the very foundations of their faith and their Christian tradition.[1] Their opponents were a varied group of theologians to be found in most of the principal Christian denomina-

---

[1]   See Harriet A. Harris, *Fundamentalism and Evangelicals* (Oxford: Oxford University Press, [1998] 2007). Her conclusions are conveniently summarised in her final chapter and in the appendix, pp. 313–36. Also James Barr, *Fundamentalism* (London: SCM Press, 1981), and Hans Küng and Jürgen Moltmann (eds.), *Concilium* (1992/93).

tions, who were commonly referred to as 'modernists' and who accepted the Higher Criticism of the Bible along with evolutionary theories in science, and suspect views on morality. In contrast to them, Christian fundamentalists typically hold a very strong view of the authority of the Scriptures (though they often differ widely in the justifications they give for this position) precisely because they wish to be faithful to the very basic tenets of their faith. Some Christian accounts of biblical inspiration closely parallel some Muslim views of the Qur'an: both groups insist that the texts themselves clearly assert that they are directly inspired by God. 'The Word of God' means what it says. Other Christian fundamentalists will also hold that the texts are guaranteed to be free from error; but they will do so on the rather different grounds that the factual assertions in the texts can be verified by historical or archaeological research. Still other believers, Christian and Muslim alike, will hold that within strict limits specified in the texts themselves some adaptation to changing circumstances can be made; but they will still totally reject the kind of scholarship typical of much of the higher criticism, which raised and still does raise fundamental questions about the authorship and literary genre of passages in the Qur'an or the various books of the Bible. Still other Christian fundamentalists pride themselves on adhering to what they would describe as the literal sense of the biblical accounts of creation, the virgin birth, the atonement through Christ's death on the cross and his bodily resurrection. These 'fundamentals' of Christian faith are not to be undermined by any modern literary theories about what texts – any texts, whether biblical texts or works such as *Hamlet* or *Finnegan's Wake* – might mean, or by any of the fashionable doubts which modern critics might wish to cast on whether we could ever discover what St Paul or an evangelist meant by what he wrote.

So it will be helpful at the outset to try to give some account of how I shall understand the term 'fundamentalism'. First, some disclaimers. I am not trying to deal with the political movements commonly described as 'fundamentalist' other than indirectly, in so far as their political behaviour is justified by strictly religious considerations. Nor am I trying to single out believers in any particular denomination or religion – there can be and have been fundamentalists who are Catholics, Baptists, Evangelicals, Muslims and Hindus. I hope that any believers who are not Christians, but have the patience to read these pages in which most of the examples are taken from Christianity, might well find their own parallels to the issues discussed here.

Two psychologists of religion have defined the term very helpfully:

> By 'fundamentalism' we mean the belief that there is one set of religious teachings that clearly contains the fundamental, intrinsic, basic, essential, inerrant truth about humanity and deity; that this essential truth is fundamentally opposed by forces of evil which must be vigorously fought; that this truth must be followed today according to the fundamental, unchangeable practices of the past; and that those who believe and follow these fundamental teachings have a special relationship to the deity.[2]

This is intended as a definition of 'religious fundamentalism', as the authors make clear. I am willing to use the term more broadly rather than restricting it to certain groups of religious believers. As I shall use it, a person can be a fundamentalist Marxist, or member of the Labour Party, or fundamentalist about the dress code for the Long Room at Lords, or for examinations at the University of Oxford. The key point is that, though I am primarily interested in religious fundamentalism, I do not think that fundamentalism in general is essentially a matter of the *content* of a person's belief system or code of practice. It is partly a matter of the attitude which people take towards that system of beliefs or practices, and partly a matter of the grounds on which that system seeks to defend itself and rebut the criticisms of it made by those 'outside'. The attitudes and, I shall argue, the means by which fundamentalists seek to defend their attitudes are by and large the same almost irrespective of the particular topics about which they have these views.

In particular, fundamentalists place a great deal of emphasis on tradition and on the importance of being faithful to that tradition. Of course, one can, and I would think that most people do, believe

---

[2]   Bob Altemyer and Bruce Hunsberger, 'Authoritarianism, religious fundamentalism, quest and prejudice', *International Journal for the Psychology of Religion* 2(2), pp. 113–33.

in the value and importance of traditions without being fundamentalist about them. What I take to be specific to fundamentalists is the way in which they commonly regard some tradition(s) as both important to their well-being and as under threat and in urgent need of defence. Those traditions must somehow be put, and indeed seen to be put, beyond criticism or reassessment.

In general, it seems that all fundamentalists believe that respect for an important tradition is threatened by some feature or other of the contemporary scientific, moral, political or intellectual climate, which calls in question either the authority of the text, or the traditional interpretation of the text, or the necessity of the practice, or all of these. Key features, on which the tradition essentially depends, are imperilled or altogether lost. So, for example, it might be felt that once the Higher Critics are let loose on the Bible, the very foundations of Christian faith are eroded; or, unless stringent tests for citizenship are insisted upon, Europe will lose its identity; if some traditional moral views are abandoned as inadequate for our modern age, the entire fabric of society will inevitably collapse. Or, quite in general, if we listen to all these modern theories of how ancient texts such as the Bible or the Qur'an are to be understood, the very basis of any religious belief will be undermined.

Fundamentalists respond in various ways to such threats. They can try to meet the threat head on, by arguing that their views – Creationism, or Intelligent Design, for example – can be harmonised with the scientific evidence just as well as stories about the Big Bang or the evolution of species. They can dispute entire methods of interpretation – for instance 'the historical-critical method' – or attack the more detailed conclusions of those scholars who argue that biblical texts often make no claim to be stating historical facts, or that the precise meanings of ancient texts are of necessity going to remain to some extent uncertain. But defence along these lines is fraught with difficulties, since it involves flying in the face of arguments which are certainly very strong. The alternative strategy is a kind of displacement. Elements in the tradition are selected which are not directly threatened by such theories, and fidelity to the tradition is redefined in terms of just those elements. Hence there are conservative traditionalists who focus upon the precise performance of special rites, or upon specific criteria for membership of the group, or upon some moral crusade, or some kind of authoritarian guarantee of orthodoxy which does not itself rely upon argument or evidence. Edmund Farley, describing these features as 'mediations', puts the matter very well:

> *Stressed by the experience of a radically secularizing diaspora of religion, some religious leaders suppress religion's perennial awareness of the limitations and fallibilities of its mediations and this is what constitutes the fundamentalist response to the modern. The fundamentalist phenomenon, then, despite its constant appeals to God and its declared intent to be God's people, do what God wants, believe what God believes, is a kind of atheism in this respect. To the extent that the holy is suppressed or displaced, fundamentalism, paradoxically, is itself a sign of religion undergoing secularisation.[3]*

Many fundamentalists would, of course, object strongly to this allegation about the ultimate implications of their whole approach, their 'meta-theology' so to speak. They would argue that, far from resulting in a kind of sacrosanct atheism, their view of how theology ought and ought not to be conducted is alone going to be able to safeguard religious values in a predominantly hostile world. Any attempt to dialogue with (to put it nicely) or parley with (with its suggestions of somewhat dishonourable compromise) contemporary culture can end only in subjecting God's revelation to mere human opinions – changeable human fashions – about what is 'acceptable in this day and age'. This challenge is not lightly to be dismissed by someone who, like myself, believes fundamentalism to be indefensible. The only way to meet the fundamentalists' criticisms is to show that respect for tradition, which is what they most value, need not involve the kind of rigidity which they regard as the only sure guarantee of fidelity. It is the aim of this book to suggest ways in which this might be done.

---

[3] Edward Farley, 'Fundamentalism: a theory', *Cross Currents* (Fall 2005), vol. 55, no. 3.

1

Tradition and Translation

Fundamentalists and their critics can easily agree on two points.

The first is that quite in general it is foolhardy to abandon traditions as though they had nothing to teach us. Indeed some of our traditions are not simply practices from which we might have a good deal to learn, but are in a stronger sense authoritative. An obvious example would be our tradition of the 'common law'. For centuries courts have applied themselves to a wide variety of difficult disputes and have tried to arrive at acceptable solutions. Moreover, courts have often been asked to assess the ways in which their predecessors have performed this task. Precedents are established, interpretations of legal texts are taken as authoritative, and yet it is nevertheless possible that changes in circumstances might call for those decisions to be revisited and possibly revised or overturned. Other traditions are authoritative in different ways and to varying degrees. There are traditions enshrined in the British way of life, in the many different rituals for marriage and other rites of passage in different cultures, in sacred texts such as the Bible, the Qur'an and the Vedas, in the proper way to conduct scientific experiments and submit them to peer review, or, less precisely, in the ideals of European civilisation, or the American way of life. One way or another, we have all been brought up to respect the traditions of the societies and professional groups to which we belong, since those traditions provide the very framework within which we can construct our own personal identities, organise our ways of conducting our affairs, and in general benefit from the wisdom of our predecessors and ancestors.

Secondly, fundamentalists and their critics can agree that if one wishes to be faithful to a tradition, it is clearly essential to have a correct understanding of what that tradition is – its origins, what its texts say, what its practices mean – and to have procedures for determining what those meanings are when disagreements about them arise. It is obviously the case that if a tradition is valued, it is valued for what it has been and still is. A traditional text, or a traditional practice, or indeed any traditional claim about what is to be taken as valuable or true, is useless in default of a clear understanding about the actual content of such a claim.

These points of agreement, however, do nothing to disguise the many differences in the ways in which fundamentalists and their critics seek to go on from there. Gaining the accurate understanding which, it is agreed, one must have is often enough a much more complex task than might at first sight appear. Typically, fundamentalists and their critics will have very different views on this point, with the critics emphasising the complexity of the quest for understanding the tradition and its origins, and fundamentalists trying to demonstrate that a proper understanding can be reached quite readily. They need to eliminate any kind of threatening complexity right at the start. Moreover, the differences of opinion about the true meaning of traditional texts and customs will often in practice become entangled with what might at first sight seem like an entirely different dispute about how we are to understand fidelity to a tradition. It will be rare to find anyone who believes that fidelity to tradition requires absolutely *no* adaptation of that tradition to the needs of its contemporary adherents. At the very least, for instance, there is often the need to translate the texts in which truths are traditionally taught; traditional practices have to be sensitively and carefully interpreted, and proper procedures for doing so must be laid down. But, of course, as soon as words like 'translation' and 'interpretation' and 'proper procedures' are introduced into the very notion of understanding fidelity to a tradition, some fundamentalists will at once feel that the pass has already been sold and the betrayal presented as a fait accompli. Indeed I myself shall presently be arguing that translation is a far from straightforward activity. In general, then, respectful adaptation presupposes that one has good reasons sometimes for accepting, sometimes for denying, that what is traditional must somehow be adapted to fit the changing circumstances of one's own times. Even if adaptation is considered to be a good thing in principle, disputes about exactly what might have to be altered to meet our modern requirements are not going to be easy to resolve. To complicate matters further, the issue about how to arrive at a correct understanding of the meaning of tradition will routinely be interwoven with the apparently different question about the degree of authority which tradition, once rightly understood, is to have. What will seem to one person to be clearly an appropriate adaptation of tradition to meet the needs of our times will seem to another to be little or nothing short of an abandonment of all that is valuable; instead of exhibiting respect for tradition, when it comes down to it such accommodations will appear to amount to a denial that tradition has any authority at all. I shall argue that it is essential to keep issues about correct interpretation and issues about the authoritativeness of tradition as distinct as possible.

As a general model for thinking about how we are to learn from tradition, I propose to examine the practice of translation; and, more particularly, to use some of the problems involved in translation as illustrations precisely because they have little or nothing directly to do with the 'hot' issues of religious disputes. I do so in the conviction that when important personal or religious issues are at stake, it is very hard to discuss the importance of tradition without one's personal involvement skewing the discussion. Much better, then, to start with more neutral issues which can more easily be examined purely on their merits, and then to argue that conclusions reached about those issues can usefully be applied to other matters where we are much more deeply involved. I hope that looking at the theory of translation will provide such a (comparatively) neutral starting point.

The aim will then be to apply the lessons learned from translation in this neutral setting to different spheres of religious tradition. The application is immediate where religious traditions rely upon texts which are taken as authoritative; for traditional religious texts commonly have to be translated if they are to be used at all. But I shall argue that the translation model has a wider application. As well as being an account of what happens in the use of texts, the account can be applied to translation in a broader sense: for the fundamentalist will often, indeed usually, wish to be faithful to *the same ways of behaving* as are to be found in the original ideal – the behaviour of Christ or of the early Christians, or the life of the Prophet – and they will have a particular version of what such fidelity will require. So the account of what translation involves can be used very widely to illuminate what is involved in learning from tradition in the spheres of ethics, liturgical and other religious practices, and even, I shall suggest, in dealing with the interactions between religion and science. In short, the question is, how can we give a faithful translation of our various religious traditions into the languages and cultures of our contemporary world? I shall endeavour to show that the various versions of fundamentalism embody mistaken theories of translation, and hence untenable views on what it is to understand and to be faithful to one's traditions.

I shall then endeavour to show how it is that translation theory can also account for what it is for a tradition to be authoritative. In so doing, I hope to complete the project of offering a balanced view of what is involved in being faithful to any authoritative tradition, without having to resort to the indefensible claims of many fundamentalists.

2

The Pitfalls of Translation

In this chapter, then, I propose to explore the process of translating from one language into another, and hence to explain why it is not a simple matter to know what is to count as a 'faithful translation' of the original. It will appear that it is easier to say what will *not* suffice as a translation policy. I shall maintain that the positive steps which must be taken to ensure fidelity reveal that translation is an art rather than a mechanical procedure. I hope that the examples which I offer here will avoid all religious or theological controversy, the better to provide a neutral approach to the highly emotive questions involving fundamentalism in the fields of religion or politics.

A faithful translation? Some illustrative examples

What exactly is a faithful translation? As I have suggested, the answer to this question is not a simple one. But to reduce the complications at least a little, we can start by assuming that we are talking about translating from some other language into our own, and that 'our own' language here will be contemporary British English. So we say that the aim of translation is to express in contemporary British English what has been said in the foreign language from which we want to translate. But there are two ways in which this apparently obvious aim might be understood:

1   The aim is to produce an English sentence which as far as possible reproduces the character of the original when it is spoken in similar circumstances by the foreigner.
2   The aim is to produce the English sentence which a speaker of British English would spontaneously use when wishing to express what the member of the foreign culture would be saying when they use their sentence.

These two apparently similar aims might lead to quite different results, however. In the table below I offer 'translations' of various proverbs from a variety of foreign cultures, designed to illustrate the tensions which arise when these two translation policies are each taken seriously. On the left there are sayings from Spanish, Italian, German, Zulu and Japanese. I have offered a verbal translation, as nearly word-for-word as I can manage: and I have offered (or suggested) what I think a native English speaker might spontaneously say in the circumstances in which the foreigner might have used the original. I have tried, where I can think of one, to provide an English proverb or familiar saying, on the grounds that ideally a proverb is best translated by finding an equivalent proverb; where the foreigners use one of theirs, it would be natural to try to find one of ours. A quick glance at the result will at once reveal that sometimes it was not at all easy to find one, and sometimes I simply could not find that kind of equivalent at all.

The most obvious result of this policy is that the versions in the second and third columns are often markedly different from one another. Why should this be so? In the examples I have listed under 'Easy', it is relatively easy to see why the difference is comparatively unproblematic. We can readily understand the situation which the verbal equivalent describes; and from our own experience we are at once likely to spot which feature of that situation is the key one on which the proverb or saying focuses. So, in each of the first two examples two good things are on offer, and anyone would want to have both of them if they could; but that is just not possible. We British, like the Spanish, have often had the experience of children at a fair or a carnival or a fiesta wanting to do everything at once; we are in general well aware of the need to keep a watch on our belongings when we would like to be cooling off in the sea. In those respects, life in Spain is not so different from life in Britain. The details of the situations which our two cultures use to illustrate the dilemma – a fiesta in Seville, a beach on the Costa del Sol, or an afternoon tea party in Tunbridge Wells – are picturesque, but relatively unimportant. Hence our equivalent proverb is ready to hand. No translation problems here; we can understand a word-for-word translation, as well as produce our own idiomatic response to the same type of situation.

Translating proverbs and sayings

Original	Verbal equivalent	Proposed idiomatic equivalent
Easy		
No se puede tocar las campanas y marchar en la procesión.	You can't toll the bells and walk in the procession.	*You can't have your cake and eat it.*
Querer nadar y guardar la ropa.	Wanting to swim and keep an eye on the clothes.	*Wanting to have one's cake and eat it.*
Indlela ibuzwa kwabaphambili.	The way forward is asked from those in front.	*The best advice comes straight from the horse's mouth.*
Ingane engakhali ifa.	The child in the back-pouch that does not cry dies.	*If there's anything you need, be sure to ask.*
More difficult		
Non si piú avere la botta piena e la moglia ubrica.	You cannot have a full cellar and a drunk wife.	*You can't have your cake and eat it.*
Revolver Roma con Santiago.	To mix Rome and Santiago.	*To set the cat among the pigeons.* or *Like a red rag to a bull.*
A quien madruga, Dios le ayuda.	God helps the one who gets up early.	*The early bird catches the worm.* or *God helps those who help themselves.*
Ithemba kalibulali.	Hope does not kill.	*I'll get there in the end.*
Damit wird der Hund in der Pfanne verrückt!	At that, the dog in the frying-pan goes mad!	*That's simply the last straw!*
Nearly Impossible!		
Isifuba esakhatshwa lidube.	His chest was kicked by a horse.	*He just can't keep his mouth shut.*
Das Kind Gottes in der Hutschachtel!	God's child in the hatbox.	*What on earth next?!*
Icala loembula ingubo lingene.	The law-suit opens the blanket and gets in.	*Don't think you've managed to get away with it!*
Unyawo alulampumulo.	The leg has no nose.	*You never know whom you might come across.*
Se ni hara wa kaerarenu.	Your stomach cannot be changed into your back.	*Necessity knows no law.*
Ngishaye esentwala.	I am patting the lice.	*Thank you; that was a lovely meal.*

We might have to think just a little longer about the third example. But here again, it depends upon an experience which is common in all cultures, which is why it does not take *too* long to figure it out. Of course if one is looking for advice it is sensible to consult people who are likely to know at first hand, so to speak. I think the phrase 'from the horse's mouth' expresses this in English, though to be honest, I am not entirely sure why it does so. It just might be because the best advice about the form of a racehorse comes from its trainer, the person closest to it. Or, perhaps, is it rather that best of all would be the view of the horse itself, if only it could speak? Or is it that the state of a horse's teeth is the best index of its age and health, and hence of its general form? Since this is somewhat complicated, I imagine that a Zulu would find it harder to see the point of the English phrase – and an English-speaker find it harder to explain it – than it is for us to see the point of the Zulu one. On the other hand, the point of the Zulu proverb about the unhappy child is at once obvious. Every culture has the experience of children whose needs are often very pressing, and expects them to make their needs known so that they can be dealt with. In all these 'easy' cases, we can at once recognise the pattern in the experiences which the two cultures share, and readily see the point of the verbally equivalent translation. Perhaps my 'idiomatic' alternative is not quite right, though: for I have assumed that the proverb is not saying something which applies only to children; and on that point I may be mistaken. But if I am right, then we too will readily be able to find a piece of folk wisdom which expresses that precise point in our own way.

The examples which I have listed as 'more difficult' are so for a variety of reasons. Sometimes it is not completely beyond dispute whether or not the imagery is merely incidental to the point being made. Is it important that the value of getting up early is explicitly related to God's assistance in the Spanish proverb, whereas we British focus on the bird finding breakfast by its own unaided efforts? My first translation assumes the reference to God is pictur-esque rather than significant, just as the religious difference between processions and tea parties was not the key issue in the earlier example. But someone might try to make the case that it is precisely the integration of human effort with *God's* assistance which is the important part of the Spanish saying. They might urge a similar point in the saying about Rome and Santiago; is it that religious differences, indeed friction, between two important religious centres are specifically mentioned because they are especially likely to be hard to handle? Here again, as with the bird and the worm, the English saying invokes nature-watchers rather than disputatious theologians. But yet again, it seems to me that *that* difference is no more than incidental; the religious imagery is more at home in Spain, perhaps: but I feel it would be over-interpreting to say that the Spanish are insisting on some theological point which the English are simply ignoring. 'Dios mio!', like 'My God!' may, but commonly does not, have any religious connotations at all. Can this uncertainty be definitively resolved? Perhaps not, or not always. Translation is an art, not an exact science. It depends upon a feel for nuance and emphasis.

The saying about the drunken wife is difficult for a different kind of reason. When we speak of having cake and eating it, or walking in procession and having fun up the tower tolling bells, *both* alternatives clearly are desirable, and it is unfortunate that we can't have both. I asked a native speaker of Italian why it is that the two alternatives in the Italian proverb – a full cellar or a drunken wife – do *not* seem both to be attractive. The explanation suggested – with some embarrassment, I think – was that anyone would of course approve of having a full cellar; and perhaps also would find a slightly tipsy wife to be more amorously inclined than if she were cold sober. If something like that is correct, then my translation will stand well enough. But since I do not share that second assumption, or at least since it did not occur to me that anyone would make it, I simply did not understand what the Italian proverb means until it was explained to me.

The remaining two 'more difficult' examples are clear enough – at any rate once they have been explained. Still, the purely verbal rendering in each case is far from clear and for that reason, if for no other, is simply inadequate as a translation. How about my more idiomatic suggestions, then? Not great, I have to admit. The German saying about the dog in the frying pan is surely humorous – black humour if you like – precisely because the situation described is so manifestly absurd. The English reference to the overloaded camel presents the situation as hinging on cruelty in a way in which the German does not, because the German is deliberately absurd; the English imagery relies on sympathy rather than absurdity. Perhaps we might notice that we too can say 'out of the frying pan into the fire', when the situation is not so serious that amusement would be quite out of place; but we would not use that expression to describe a failed escape which was truly tragic. So 'out of the frying pan …' has, to my ear at least, something of the same half-humour as the German saying about the dog in the frying pan, though its point is quite different. Perhaps, then, my translation of the German saying, with overtones of pity for the poor camel rather than amusement about a rather absurd disaster, is less than accurate? Not so easy to decide, except to say that I don't think I can do any better.

What does emerge very clearly from these examples is that faithful translation requires more than a knowledge of the grammar and vocabulary of the foreign language. It requires a knowledge of the two cultures involved and a feel for which aspects of situations are the ones on which each culture would naturally focus. The very possibility of translation depends upon the fact that there are many situations which are common to the two cultures, and indeed the human predicament quite generally. These are just the kind of situations upon which folk wisdom is likely to focus, even though different images are used to make the same point. The translator will not always have that knowledge immediately ready to hand, so a good translation will not always be readily available despite her ability to render every single word correctly into her own language.

The group of sayings which I have labelled 'nearly impossible' illustrate this to a much greater degree. Here, the verbally equivalent renderings are almost completely unintelligible; and, as such, I would argue that they simply cannot count as translations at all. If mutual understanding is to be achieved, a great deal of help will be required, and considerable negotiation. What exactly *is* the point about being kicked by a horse in the chest? Shocked astonishment? Severe and totally unforeseen pain? Neither, I am told. The point of the comparison is that when someone is kicked hard in the chest, all their breath is forcibly expelled: hence the connection with being unable to keep a secret, spilling the beans, or being a blabbermouth. I cannot think of a suitable contemporary idiom which focuses precisely upon the inability to hold one's breath. ('Don't hold your breath', meaning 'Don't hang about waiting expectantly for too long!' plainly won't do here.) Perhaps one might try something like 'It's no use telling him not to breathe a word – he can't help it!' Is that a paraphrase rather than a translation? The problem is yet worse with 'God's child in the hatbox'. The image, I am told, is that of a charming child ('God's child', after all!) who has found his Edwardian mother's huge hatbox, into which over the years she has dumped all kinds of odds and ends. The child is inside it, tossing out a random collection of articles one at a time: the amused and perhaps slightly apprehensive or even embarrassed mother has absolutely no idea what will turn up next. 'What on earth next!', which is my attempted translation, gets the point all right; but it totally lacks the vivid imagery; and it also lacks the sense of amused bewilderment unless it were to be said in just the right tone of voice, and in just the right circumstances, because it contains no image to set the tone. The German text does not in itself specify the precise circumstances, nor, of course, can a text always convey the appropriate tone of voice. So my translation is rather pale by comparison, and even then was arrived at only after some conversation between myself and a German-speaker about the households of well-to-do families before the First World War. It is not that bewildered amusement is not shared by the two cultures: it is rather that the saying itself does not bring sufficient context with it. In contrast, perhaps, the Zulu saying about the blanket is a bit clearer. The blanket is a symbol of security and safeness, yet a snake or a scorpion can crawl in under one's blanket nonetheless: so the criminal will have to reckon on being caught, even when he is most confident that he has safely escaped prosecution. But I can find no suitable image in our culture: so my translation, which is colloquial enough and accurate as far as it goes, totally lacks the vividness of the original.

I found the last three on my list the least intelligible of all. My best shot at 'The leg has no nose' was that each part of the body needs the other parts: perhaps, then, an exhortation to mutual co-operation? 'Two heads are better than one', maybe, or 'Many hands make light work'? Not so, it appears. The function of the leg is to take one from place to place, and that of the nose to scent out in advance, as an animal might, what one is going to meet as one goes along. The saying can be used either as a warning – 'You never know who might be lying in wait for you!' along similar lines to the previous saying about the snake in the blanket; but if the context is right, it could equally be said in an encouraging tone of voice, 'Just go – you never know whom you might meet!'

The Japanese proverb 'Your stomach cannot be changed into your back' relies on the point that the stomach, containing as it does so many important organs, is not a sensible exchange even for something as vital as one's back; yet in an extremity one should be willing to sacrifice even one's back to protect one's stomach. The most dreadful choices still have to be faced, and one might have to do what would normally be unthinkable. The idiomatic translation was suggested to me, with some hesitation, by the Japanese to whom I owe the original example. I myself could have got nowhere near it.

Again, left to myself, I could make absolutely nothing of the final example. And once again, the key was a fact about the rural Ndebele village in which it might have been said. In such a village body lice would be common. So, if one pats one's stomach after a meal, one is likely also to be patting the lice on one's body. The saying is therefore a way of expressing thanks for a thoroughly lovely and satisfying meal. The gesture of patting itself is the same as it might be here in Britain, and is natural enough; but the description is not one which would be connected with that gesture other than in the particular circumstances of rural Southern Africa.

So what is to be learned from the problems for translators which these examples pose? I suggest the following:

1   When one has succeeded in translating, it will be because one has managed to identify an interest, or type of predicament, or a piece of sensible advice which would be shared between the foreign culture and our own.

2   A point which is obvious in this context will, as we shall see, turn out to be a crucial point later: it is important to realise what kind of texts these are – they are proverbs, or sayings. They are not setting out to describe the behaviour of early birds or worms, or people patting lice. They use those images to convey something quite different. Many failures to understand traditional Christian texts derive from just such a failure to recognise the function of the texts involved.

3   The situation used to exemplify such a shared perception
    may vary widely depending upon the circumstances of
    the two cultures involved. It may even be that many
    members of a culture can no longer identify precisely why
    a particular phrase is used in that way – I have no idea
    why people in Manchester will say in native Mancunian,
    'I'll go to the bottom of our stairs!' to express astonish-
    ment, for example.[1] Taken at face value, this is unintelli-
    gible to a speaker of standard English. Word-for-word
    literalism is often completely useless as a translation
    procedure.

4   Cultural gaps can vary in width. Where they are less wide,
    the verbal equivalence will be useless as a translation; where
    they are less wide, the verbal equivalent can, once it has been
    explained, make sense; but would still be sufficiently far
    from our own usage as not to be acceptable as a translation,
    since a reader who has not been given the clue could well
    totally fail to understand, even though it is obvious enough
    once an adequate commentary has been provided.

5   In the easy cases, how are we to choose between using the
    verbal equivalent and using an existing expression in one's
    own language – between 'You cannot toll the bells and walk
    in the procession' and 'You cannot have your cake and eat
    it'? I think there are two issues in such cases. If what one is
    interested in is to explain the original in its context, then the
    verbal equivalent (with or without commentary as neces-
    sary) is likely to be better, since it remains in that original
    setting as far as possible. On the other hand, if the aim of
    translation is to communicate and to make the same point in
    a way which would fit into the usage of our culture, rather
    than to initiate a seminar in cross-cultural curiosities, then
    an idiomatic translation is surely required.

6   In the more difficult and in the 'nearly impossible' cases it is
    more challenging, but all the more essential, to try to find an
    idiomatic translation, since nothing else will really be intel-

[1]   See Nigel Rees, *Oops! Pardon Mrs Arden: An Embarrassment of Domestic Catch-
    phrases* (London: Robson Books, 2001), pp. 99–100, where he gives various possible
    and widely different suggestions.

ligible at all without having to produce a commentary on every occasion it is to be used.

I have used proverbs and sayings to introduce these points about translation, since they provide obvious and interesting examples of issues which are in fact quite general. What is important to notice is that translation *always* involves some intercultural negotiation, ideally between people who are at least somewhat familiar with each other's culture. Sometimes the negotiation will be comparatively quick and easily concluded; at other times one person may try to explain the point of the imagery or the overtones of a word, and the person who is looking for the translation will then have to consider possible alternatives; what is then likely to ensue is a series of exchanges until both parties feel as satisfied as they can be that a reasonable equivalence has been found. What is important is to realise that invoking notions such as 'faithfulness to the original' does nothing to solve whatever problems there may be. Of course a good translation has to be faithful to the original; but for that very reason it has to be intelligible; and as far as possible it is desirable that it be something which the people to whom it is offered would understand and feel at home with when trying to express their own thoughts. To be faithful to the original is to produce something which in those ways functions as comfortably as did the original. 'Fidelity to the original' certainly is not in itself an argument in favour of a word-for-word verbal equivalent; it could lead to that only in the easiest cases. Translation is an art, and cannot be reduced to any simple formula which would automatically guarantee success.

Reaching across culture gaps

There are further difficulties which are not illustrated so clearly by the difficulties of translating proverbs and sayings.

How can we understand the ancients?

The main difficulty posed by ancient texts is simply that they are ancient. The fact that they come to us as written rather than spoken makes many of the nuances just mentioned potentially much more difficult, though certainly not always impossible, to detect. It is also the case that there are likely to be quite a few words to which at best only a very general sense can be assigned by making an inference from the context – for instance, that it must mean some kind of bird – a shrike, bustard or kestrel – or some part of a ship – a halyard, futtock or transom – but we can't be more precise than that. There will sometimes be idioms which we simply cannot fathom at all. More seriously, there is no living interlocutor with whom the contemporary translator can negotiate, exchanging versions of what each other is saying until there is mutual agreement that a suitable equivalent has been discovered.

Still, there are ways in which most of these handicaps can be overcome, especially when, as is the case nowadays with almost all the ancient texts from Greece, Rome, Egypt, Mesopotamia and Palestine, there are many sources from which we can learn, and many ways in which light can be shed on them by studying texts from neighbouring civilisations.[2] These parallels function somewhat as living interlocutors do when we are translating from a contemporary language into our own. Given all that we can learn even about ancient languages, through linguistics, etymology, archaeology and history, the normal position is that we can come to understand them well enough to translate them with a high degree of accuracy. But 'accuracy', as I have already argued above, is not a quality which can be assessed by applying rules unthinkingly; translation programmes for computers can succeed only to a very limited extent. Translation is not a mechanical procedure; it is an art.

Can we ever 'reach' others?

It is often a difficult art, as I have been trying to point out. Nevertheless I hope it will be clear from my preceding remarks that I see no reason to accept the more sceptical view not infrequently asserted by some contemporary literary critics. They argue that we cannot possibly be in a position to discover the meaning of an ancient text, or indeed that even to speak of '*the* meaning' of any text is simply a crude mistake. All one can aspire to is to know

---

[2]   There are exceptions: in the case of the language known as Linear A, found on tablets discovered in Crete, our best efforts have so far failed completely. We do not even know to which family of languages it belongs.

'what that text says to me'. Such critics often point to the extraordinary complexity of the human mind and the fact that the emotional, literary, cultural and personal background of any speaker is difficult for another person to know with any accuracy or detail. They then argue that we cannot possibly now hope to discover the intention 'inside' the mind of an ancient writer, yet it is that intention which determines the meaning of what the person said. The intentions even of our contemporaries are inevitably opaque to us; so, they argue, how much more will that limit our grasp of what was in the mind of ancient writers when they produced their texts? True enough: what made someone say something, what associations their words might have had for them, what they hoped another person might pick up from what they said – all these things may be only partially obvious from what they said and how they said it. Nonetheless I think that this view of ancient texts, or indeed of any text, is unduly pessimistic. The intelligibility of what anyone says depends upon a set of conventions to which speakers have all subscribed; and the strong presumption is that in speaking or writing they intend to observe these shared conventions. Only a Humpty Dumpty can pretend that the meanings of the words he uses are controlled by his intentions.[3] Meaning is public, rather than personal. Moreover, in our present context, it is to be noted that such a sceptical account of meaning is inconsistent with any view of an ancient text being authoritative; for what such a text might happen to convey to me might have nothing whatever to do with what the original authoritative author had in mind.

The perils of extremism

How one gets in touch: the professional translator

I have been arguing for what I consider to be a moderate centrist position about what it is to be able to give a faithful translation of

---

[3]   The theory is pilloried by Lewis Carroll, in *Alice through the Looking Glass*, ch. 6.

'When *I* use a word,' Humpty Dumpty said, in a rather scornful tone, 'it means just what I choose it to mean, neither more nor less.'

'The question is,' said Alice, 'whether you *can* make words mean so many different things.'

'The question is,' said Humpty Dumpty, 'which is to be master – that's all.'

There follows a masterpiece of nonsensical exegesis, a salutary warning to some modern theorists.

what someone has written or said. In particular, I have been arguing that any professional translator will in practice hold the following views:

1   That there is a meaning to what has been written or said which can be grasped and used as the basis for a good translation. It is also quite possible for someone to misunderstand a text, and hence to fail to translate it correctly.
2   However, even when one has correctly understood what has been said in a foreign language, it does not at all follow that translation will then be easy; and, when one is dealing with vivid imagery, it may not always be possible to produce a translation which is both idiomatic, intelligible, and uses the same or equally vivid imagery.
3   What a text means is defined in terms of what a person with the relevant linguistic competence would understand by it in its original context. Though linguistic competence can be described in general terms, it cannot, I believe, be defined in terms of rules or conventions whose correct application in individual circumstances needs no further thought or judgement. Linguistic competence is an artistic skill, not the ability to carry out a mechanical procedure.
4   What a text means depends on the shared conventions of the time and in the context in which it was produced: it does *not* depend on whether *we* take it to be true, helpful, outlandish or deeply meaningful. A faithful translation may equally well express something which to our ears is shocking, clearly mistaken, inspiring, or simply puzzling.

This position can be contrasted with extreme positions in both directions.

In touch with what? Postmodern scepticism

The postmodernist would regard as quite unrealistic the model of dialogue with which I began, when I suggested that successful translation depends upon an intercultural negotiation process, and that a faithful translation has been found when both parties to the negotiation are satisfied with the outcome. The key postmodern move is to point out that both parties to such a negotiation will inevitably bring their own individual standpoints, assumptions, cultural biases and preoccupations to the negotiating table. As a result, it is not just that they might find it hard to agree on an outcome; there is an important sense in which neither the starting point nor the outcome (if there were to be one) can be described as 'the same' for both parties. At every stage, each will be interpreting what the other is saying in their separate ways; to search for a neutral standpoint from which the original can be understood, or a proposed translation assessed, is to pursue a will-o'-the wisp. Rather than dealing with a shared text – whether written or spoken – any person will be dealing only with a text-as-it-affects-a-given-reader. We cannot expect to arrive at a shared view of 'the meaning'. Such a 'meaning' would be owned by nobody. Each person will indeed search for meaning in a text; but this aim, too, can be interpreted in two ways. In the stronger sense, the text will only come to 'mean something' for the interpreter when the interpreter finds important, or approves of, what they take it to say; if it 'means nothing to them' then they will deem it untranslatable. In the weaker sense they might concede that while in their own way they can make sense of it, it is still of no use to them. The key contention of the postmodernist, then, is:

5   The meaning of any text cannot be distinct from the interpretation given to it by each different reader/hearer; and that interpretation will depend upon their own individual backgrounds, cultures and interests. There is no possibility of understanding a text 'from a neutral standpoint', and then describing that understanding as *the* meaning.

This is inconsistent with (4) above; and from this contention it seems to me to follow that

6   No one person's interpretation is preferable to that of anyone else. The text 'itself' cannot be appealed to in order to validate one rather than another interpretation. One cannot 'misunderstand' or 'mistranslate'. This is inconsistent with (1) above.

It is of course true that readers will inevitably, and quite properly, bring to texts their own background of information, culture, historical understanding and so forth. To that extent, a neutral understanding of the meaning of the original text is going to be an ideal to which we can only approximate. But as our growing understanding of ancient texts surely shows, enormous progress can be and has been made. If the extreme postmodernist view were correct, this kind of 'progress' would have no application, presupposing as it does an ideally correct understanding to which we gradually approximate. I regard that conclusion as so out of line with what has been achieved in the way of understanding ancient texts as hardly to be worth taking seriously. Moreover, though (6) is often presented as a quite general theory of meaning, it is usually applied only to selected types of text (not, for instance, to instructions for operating the washing machine, nor directions for finding someone's house – for obvious reasons!). But no explanation is usually offered as to why radically different accounts of meaning should have to be invoked to cover the less practical cases. The postmodernist view is also, as we shall see later, a radically relativist position, and is therefore open to all the criticisms to which relativism is vulnerable. I believe it involves a quite misleading confusion between understanding what a text says, and deciding what, if anything, one might find true, or false, interesting or irrelevant, inspiring or repugnant in what that text says.

It's really very simple: the rigorist

The term 'rigorist' has many senses. Here I am using it to refer to someone who can be described as rigorist because of the view they hold about the understanding and translation of texts. Rigorists are at the opposite pole to the postmodernist. Indeed, they regard the postmodernist as having reached the bottom of the slippery slope upon which the person whom I have described as the 'professional translator' has, alas, already begun to slide. For of course the professional translator has already admitted that translation is an art, not a clear-cut matter of following the procedure; she has insisted that translating, and therefore understanding, depends on a large number of factors which she is pleased to describe as 'linguistic competence' but which seem to rigorists to be dangerously vague and unpredictable. And as my examples of 'proposed idiomatic translations' make only too clear, they will say that what one then ends up with will all too often bear little or no relation to what we were supposed to be translating. How, then, can that be an example of faithfulness to the original?

The rigorists' guiding principle, then, could be put as follows:

7 Translation, to be faithful and accurate, should contain no interpretation at all.

In practice the translator's tools should be simply a good grammar and a large dictionary of verbal equivalents; and if the dictionary yields no equivalent, as is often not infrequently the case with technical terms where accuracy is also likely to be specially important, then the safest course is to transliterate. The principle expressed in (7) is the contrary of the modernist's maxim as set out in (5) above. Rigorists would argue that their approach is uncomplicated, clear and utterly respectful of the original; indeed they might go further and counterattack, arguing that the modernist, apparently, could dispense with the original altogether and just make up a translation as he pleases; and the allegedly professional translator turns out to be a somewhat shifty character, apparently prepared to abandon the original when they find it difficult or uncongenial or try themselves to be clever or elegant.

However, despite its apparently attractive simplicity and clarity, this rigorist translation policy seems to me to pay such scant regard to the requirement that any translation has to be intelligible to the intended audience that in practice it will often be almost useless; several of my proverb examples surely make this quite clear. Moreover, rigorism simply does not account for how we actually behave when conversing with foreigners at any level more complex than the totally banal. Our differences may not be apparent when we are dealing with such simple thoughts as 'What time does the bus leave?', or 'My brother is married to a schoolteacher'. Such translations can indeed often be produced with no more than a dictionary and a grammar. But things are not as simple as the rigorist likes to suggest. The perils of such a policy even in comparatively simple cases are evident in many a menu translated for the benefit of tourists, or in the translated instructions for assembling or operating pieces of apparatus one has just bought, let alone when it comes to any attempt to translate anything more ambitious.[4] The reason is obvious enough. To look for a translation even for a simple word will much more often than not involve the translator with a choice of alternatives, as a moment's look at a dictionary will make clear. That several words can properly be offered as translations for a given word does not in the least imply that they are all synonyms of one another. Rigorism is ultimately a mirage. It is the extreme end of a spectrum of policies, of which postmodernism is at the other extreme. Where precisely one decides to come down between these two is a matter of knowledge, and above all of judgement: judgement which must consider which of several alternatives are reasonably possible, given the conventions of the languages, and which will, as a matter of policy, respond to the needs of the intended audience.

What makes cultural exchange possible?

I have suggested above that all translation involves some level of intercultural negotiation – ideally between two people each of whom has more than a minimal linguistic competence in the other language as well as being totally at home in their own. Perhaps, in addition to thinking of it as a negotiation process, which perhaps has unfortunate overtones of competitiveness, one might also think of it as a mutual learning process, Each of the persons involved has to learn from the other the nuances of meaning involved in the original text and in the possible translations. There is very often a kind of to-ing and fro-ing; a translation is proposed and the first speaker says, 'No, if we had wanted to say that, we would have said …', and so on. Between them they can communicate the 'feel' for the overtones and implications of what is being said which is essential if they are eventually to arrive at an agreed 'best fit'. Now, this procedure could not even begin were there not some reasons for supposing that there is sufficient common ground to make

---

[4]   I offer an example from a tourist website: Santa Cristina d'Aro, we are told,

> disposes of three characteristics beachs. First of all 'Cala Canyet' little beach with wharf. Second 'Cala del Sr Ramon', sand beach with services of naturist king. Third 'Cala Vallpresona', beach of little stone, without services and food access (naturist king). The village is incide of tourismcycle net and is designed for know most interesting places of our district, walking on bicycle, you can find plans of circuits in our tourist office.

In fairness I must add that the website has since been completely revised and is now in excellent English, though I also feel that something has been lost!

communication at the required level possible. It is this point which the radical postmodernist will question, and the rigorist will too easily take for granted.

Ludwig Wittgenstein said, 'The limits of my language mean the limits of my world.'[5] Here and in his later works he was drawing attention to the fact that our language, our entire way of thinking about, describing and assessing what is true in our world, cannot be separated from our way of living. To this extent the postmodernist is right: there is no 'neutral' standpoint for establishing how the world is, and we have no way of assessing the truth of things other than in terms of how we have learned to think and talk. To accept that, however, is not necessarily to accept the full-blown relativist position that there is no common ground between cultures, that we really do inhabit different 'worlds', or that we humans cannot learn to understand our one world more accurately in order to lead lives which are more fulfilling. At a most basic level, the fact that we share a common human nature means that despite our cultural and individual differences we still have our most basic needs in common, and must therefore interact with our world in ways which are at the deepest level shared. On the other hand, human beings are also the most flexible of earth's inhabitants. We can develop widely different styles of life, adapting to different climates, individual temperaments and levels of technological expertise; we can co-operate by using very different kinds of social structures; we can flourish in very different ways, as individuals and as societies. We humans speak differently, see the world differently, live differently from one another. Nevertheless, and this is crucial, our different cultures and languages of necessity have shared roots. So there simply must be a basis for shared understanding between us: even though to reach such an understanding with any accuracy will often enough take patient hard work. The following diagram illustrates the different levels of difficulty in finding translations which are faithful to the original.

There is an area which all three triangles share, which we can take as representing those features of human nature which are common to us all. This common human nature is the basis on

---

[5]   *Tractatus Logico-Philosophicus*, 5.6.

which all our languages, our ways of 'seeing the world' ultimately rest. So the diagram can also represent the relationships between three languages.

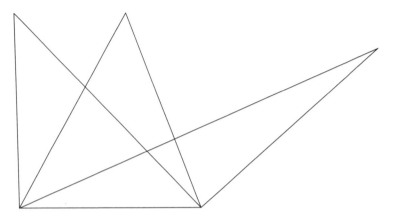

The relationship between three hypothetical cultures, each represented by a triangle

Plainly our cultures are complex and in complex ways differ from one another. The three culture-triangles in the diagram display how two different cultures might still be closer to one another than either is to a third. And the further an element in that culture is from the shared human base, the greater the distance will be from what is said in one culture to the best translation in the language of another.

The suggestion is that translation involves finding the relevant element in the shared area of overlap: thus, we all sometimes have to choose between desirable alternatives; we all need help and need to ask for it; we can all value confidentiality, or wish to thank people for a meal. Where a given remark comes in an area shared with another culture, the translation problems between them are normally small because the patterns of behaviour are very similar. The translation problems are greater the further back down one has to go to reach needs and concerns which are shared. And think of the links between the myths and fairy stories from quite different cultures, which very often despite appearance address issues which are relevant to us all.

Where what we say is highly specific to one culture (widespread infection by body lice, large Edwardian hatboxes, the loading of camels, thinking of one's nose as scenting danger afar off, to take some of the examples from the proverbs I have mentioned above) the difficulty of translation will be greater the further back down towards the base one has to travel in order to find something which is shared: and the greater the surface dissimilarity will tend to be between the original and its faithful translation.

The project again

I hope that these remarks about translation, and the examples with which I have illustrated them, are at least comparatively uncontroversial. I have deliberately drawn them from a setting in which there is no hidden theological or political or nationalist agenda, in the hope that by so doing I may use them as a tool with which various much more contentious issues involving theology, politics or national identity can be assessed with at least a considerable degree of impartiality.

My project is based on the claim that the question 'What does it mean to be faithful to a tradition?' can be illuminated by using as a model the problems of finding a suitable translation. Problems concerning how one can, or should, faithfully interpret important religious texts from one's tradition are, of course, just a special case of the issues which I have already raised: and I hope to show that there are theological and political parallels to the professional translator, the postmodernist and the rigorist whose approaches I have already outlined. It will come as no surprise which of these models I shall recommend. Less obviously, perhaps, I shall then suggest that a similar approach will illuminate what is involved in being faithful to the morality enshrined in one's tradition; the parallel with translation can helpfully be maintained in the context of actions as well as texts. 'What would that person say were they speaking in my language to me, here, today?' is, so put, a straight question about faithful translation. And 'What would that person do if they were in my situation here and now?' is in many ways similar. Both with textual and with moral traditions one is forced to confront the difficulties of intercultural negotiation, and to try to replicate as honestly as possible the gradually refined exchange which is involved in any attempt to reach an understanding between two cultures. The work of the professional translator provides a model in both cases. Perhaps least obvious of all, at first sight, are the problems in remaining faithful to a tradition when the intellectual or scientific or environmental climates are now quite different from how they were at an earlier stage of the tradition. I shall argue nevertheless that the tensions between science and religion which have been characteristic of the last two centuries can also be approached using the problems of translation as a model.

3

Beyond Mere Words

'Speech acts': what we can do with words

Speech acts in general

Understanding what someone says is not just a matter of understanding the words. If someone says to us, 'But I hoped you'd realize that I only said that because I was too shy to ask you directly', one might well reply, 'I am sorry, I just didn't pick up that that was what you wanted all along'. So a distinction has to be made. There is one sense of 'what they said' in which this kind of failure is not strictly a mistranslation of what the person's *words* mean. To understand at that level, one needs no more than to have grasped the senses of words, and the grammar and syntax and the other conventions governing the use of sentences. The further problem is quite different, and is rather to be seen as a failure to pick up what the person was *doing* in saying what they said. People commonly correct such a misunderstanding: they might say, for instance, that they were 'only joking'. The more complex example I have just given, where the person was too shy to ask directly though that is in fact what they were trying to do, is another illustration of the same point. To understand a language at the first and most basic level does not, of course, require one to be a psychotherapist specialising in treating its native speakers. Of course psychotherapists, like the rest of us, understand what their clients say at one level – the obvious and immediate level; but they are in a position to go on to help them in ways which the rest of us sometimes cannot, because they are trained to understand what their client is in fact *doing* in speaking as they do. To grasp this at any deep level requires highly complex skills. But still, all of us, at our own levels, need to be able to pick up a good deal of what people are *doing* with words.

That last point can be made more general. The philosopher J. L. Austin is famous for having introduced the notion of a 'speech act'

in his book *How to Do Things with Words*.[1] People who have
learned a language have learned a great many things which they
can do with words. At the most basic level, we can refer to and
describe things: we can say that the post-box is over there, and that
it is red. We have learned how to ask questions and to express
wishes or commands. These are all obvious examples of things we
can do with words.

But when we are thoroughly at home in a language we have
learned a great deal more: we have learned how to interpret tones of
voice. We can recognise irony and sarcasm – despite the fact that
simply using the words 'I suppose you know all about that!' does
not in itself tell us what a person who uses them is saying. Is it
sarcasm, compliment, irony? We have learned to recognise
whether a sentence which has the grammatical form of a statement,
such as 'You're going to London tomorrow', is being used to ask a
question, or to issue an order, to express astonishment, or to
communicate a proverbial saying. We have learnt how and when to
say 'I know what I am doing!' as a way of asking to be allowed to
get on without interference. Again, we have learned to use meta-
phors, and to recognise when other people are using them; so even
a philosopher who believes that minds are identical to brains will
have no trouble distinguishing between 'He gave him a piece of his
mind' and 'He gave him a piece of his brain'; the first is an
expression of disagreement or anger; the second (at a pinch!) might
describe the preliminaries to having a biopsy done. In the same
way, we will have learned to be able to distinguish jokes from
things said in all seriousness, proverbs from straightforward
descriptions, fairy tales from myths, and both of these from historical narratives. Linguistic competence is a many-faceted skill.
Some aspects of it – those depending to any great extent on tone of
voice, for instance – might be much easier to judge from a spoken
than from a written communication. 'Once upon a time' needs to be
said with a distinctive intonation if we intend to introduce a
fairy-tale, for it can also simply introduce some event from the past

[1]   J. L. Austin, *How to Do Things with Words*, ed. J. O. Urmson and Marina Sbisà, 2nd
     edn Oxford: Oxford University Press, 1975); see the subsequent elaboration of his
     view by J. Searle, *Speech Acts: An Essay in the Philosophy of Language* (Cambridge:
     Cambridge University Press, 1969; S. L. Tsohatzidis (ed.), *Foundations of Speech-Act
     Theory: Philosophical and Linguistic Perspectives* (London: Routledge, 1994).

– 'Once upon a time I used to think that!' But in general, those competent in a language will understand not merely the content of what someone is saying; they will understand what the person is doing when they say (or write) it. Foreigners will typically find such nuances more difficult to pick up even when they are well equipped grammatically and have a good vocabulary; and if an interpreter fails to pick up such aspects of what is being said, then, even when the translation is accurate enough from a purely verbal point of view, the understanding of what was said will still be more or less defective. These difficulties are considerably greater when we are dealing with a written text rather than, say, a recording where the tone of voice can be determined; or when we are dealing with an ancient text whose idioms and turns of phrase are not always easy to determine.

Three sayings of Jesus: how to take them?

There are certainly instances in sacred texts where we are confronted with just such problems of understanding. Here are three texts, all taken from Matthew's account of the Sermon of the Mount, apparently said in the same context, but where it might not be totally clear exactly what Jesus meant by them because it is not clear what *kind* of utterance they are in terms of the context and conventions of the situation in which they were said:

> '*If your right eye causes you to sin, tear it out and throw it away; it is better for you to lose one of your members than for your whole body to be thrown into hell.*
>
> '*And if your right hand causes you to sin, cut it off and throw it away; it is better for you to lose one of your members than for your whole body to be thrown into hell ...*
>
> '*You have heard it said, "An eye for an eye and a tooth for a tooth"; but I say to you, do not resist an evildoer. But if anyone strikes you on the right cheek, turn the other also.*'[2]

There have been few Christians who would regard either of the first two statements as straightforward commands. Here, it would be argued, we are dealing with rhetorical exaggeration. But there

---

[2]   Matt. 5:29–30, 38–39.

certainly have been Christian pacifists who insist that the third of
these statements is a precise command which the sincere believer is
bound to obey, and who would maintain that even in the most
extreme circumstances, pacifism and non-violent resistance is a
Christian duty.[3] Gandhi based much of his own tactic of non-
violent resistance on this interpretation of Christian teaching. So
what is one to make of the situation in which pacifist Christians
would consider themselves as being most faithful to the Lord's
command as expressed in the third text, while yet taking the two
preceding sayings to be rhetorical exaggerations for the sake of
emphasis, and who would consider as indefensibly fundamentalist
those Muslims who might take equally literally the Sharia punishment for theft? Even when the translation in the narrowest sense is
not in dispute, key issues for proper understanding of what was
said are as yet unresolved. How are we to proceed?

The types of variation to be found here suggest that the proc-
esses at work are in fact quite complex. Christians who regard both
the first two statements as rhetorical exaggerations might well
nonetheless defend the death penalty – and indeed in the not so
distant past might have defended the death penalty for comparatively trivial theft, say, of a sheep. They would doubtless have
defended this view on the grounds that the threat of death is a
powerful deterrent. But just such a defence of the saying in the
Qur'an requiring the amputation of a hand as a penalty or theft is
given by some Muslims – that such a punishment operates as a
deterrent. At least in some cases, then, they are prepared to adopt as
a straightforward moral principle a saying which others of their
own or of other faiths might find untenable if so understood; and
similar considerations apply to pacifist Christians' interpretation of
the saying on non-resistance. Whether the meaning of a sentence in
an ancient text is perfectly straightforward, rather than, say, a
rhetorical wake-up call, is rarely decided *simply* on grounds that
only in so doing can someone be faithful to their tradition. They
will defend their conclusion on wider moral grounds: and often, as
in the case of Islamic law, there are many ways in which the
severity of the extreme punishment is mitigated by the very strict

---

[3]   See Dr Hoekema, 'A practical Christian pacifism', *The Christian Century*, 22 October
1986, pp. 917–19. I discuss pacifism more at length below, p. 152.

conditions – in terms of witnesses and intent, for instance – which must be met if the accused is to be found guilty or the penalty carried out. These considerations would suggest that in moral matters people of many different faiths have frequently *not* held the characteristically fundamentalist position, that fidelity to tradition requires that traditional teaching should not be subjected to any interpretation whatsoever. Instead, they have used a variety of interpretative techniques, and their understanding will be as different from the purely lexical meaning of the text as my idiomatic translation of proverbs is from the word-for-word versions.

However, fully fundamentalist approaches to biblical moral texts are not hard to find. As Edward Farley pointed out,[4] it is typical of a fundamentalist approach to be *selective* about which elements in a tradition must be relied upon, and which can simply be unheeded. The reason is that once diverse strands of the tradition are all given their due weight, issues of interpretation, authenticity, conflicting messages and the possibility of future adaptation to circumstances at once become pressing. The fundamentalist believes that fidelity to tradition excludes any such ambiguities in interpretation, or any possibility of adapting teaching to new circumstances. It is therefore easier to solve problems by being somewhat more selective in one's choice of authorities as starting points. Thus, in the same context in Matthew's Gospel, selectivity has frequently been practised: the saying prohibiting all oaths has been almost totally ignored by most subsequent Christians; Luke's version of the prohibition on divorce and remarriage is widely taken in the Eastern Christian Churches as too restrictive; in preference they have appealed to Matthew's version which includes an exception clause to cover the case of adultery; but until very recently, Luke's stricter rule has been taken as the default position by most Western Christians and enforced without further adaptation, despite the case mentioned in Paul's letter to the Corinthians,[5] and despite the way in which in that chapter Paul distinguishes between what the Lord has said and what Paul himself advises in the circumstances with which his community is faced.

The fundamentalist ignores such complications, selects preferred texts, and refuses any further discussion of precisely which

---

[4]   Cited above, p. 5.
[5]   Matt. 5:31–32, Luke 26:18; see also 1 Cor. 7:15.

of several possible speech acts a given text exemplifies. The fundamentalist policy takes a very clear line on what it is to be faithful to a tradition, but at the cost of a radical failure to investigate the nuances and varieties of meaning within the very tradition which is taken as authoritative.

The upshot of this discussion is to suggest two things. The first is that any kind of translation which succeeds only by looking at selected parts of the original is plainly going to be incomplete. Secondly, it needs to be stressed over and over again that it is no use saying that contemporary Christianity regards the Scriptures as in some way foundational or authoritative, unless one is also willing to take the trouble – and face the perhaps at first sight unpalatable consequences – of discovering what the original text actually meant and what its writers were doing when they wrote as they did and used their sources in the ways that they did. What the text 'says' is partly a function of the sense of the words and the structures of grammar and syntax, of course: but it is at least as much dependent upon what the speakers or writers of those sentences were *doing* in writing as they did: were they being rhetorical, sarcastic, humorous, speaking figuratively, talking about ideals, issuing commands in the name of God, or intending their remarks to be understood against the background of a particular situation? Those are key questions.

Or at least, so I shall argue. The adequacy of any model as a tool of inquiry can only be assessed by results. There is no quick formula for providing good translations or accurate understanding. In the same way, fidelity to a tradition is not something which can be assessed by any simple formulaic test. In the last analysis, there is no substitute for the sense of 'fit' which shows that the intelligent search for a good translation has been a success; and we must also recall that there are cases where we may have to settle for a translation which is adequate and not misleading, even if it lacks some of the characteristic qualities of the original.

It is time to take some important examples of cases where the translation of ancient texts has proved difficult, and where the whole idea of fidelity to a tradition is problematic. To some of these I now turn.

Large-scale misunderstandings

Perhaps the first thing that springs to mind when one mentions fundamentalism in a Christian context is the controversy over the proper interpretation of the opening three chapters of the book of Genesis. I shall discuss these chapters in more detail later, when I consider the relationships between fundamentalism and the sciences. But in those chapters, as very frequently elsewhere in the Bible, readers must stop to ask themselves what a passage in the Bible is trying to do. Just as uttering an individual sentence can be a way of *doing* something (for example, performing some particular speech act which is not simply that of straightforwardly asserting something), so too much longer passages can be trying to do many different kinds of thing. The notion of a speech act can be applied to language units which are much larger than individual sentences, and include, for instance, parables, sitcoms, biographies and the kind of joke that begins 'An Englishman, a Scotsman and an Irishman ...'. All these could, in a very general way, be described as narratives – they relate one event after another. But only of the events related in a biography would it make sense to ask exactly when and where they took place.

The fundamentalist typically assumes that all narrative passages in the Bible relate events in the same way as a biography might, and fails to consider other possible ways of understanding what any particular narrative is trying to *do*. For example, the book of Job is not a description of an actual series of conversations; rather it is a dramatised discussion – a rather more poetic version of what we find in Plato's dialogues – employed as a way of dealing with the problem of evil. Why is it that the just suffer? Its opening words, 'There was a man in the land of Hus named Job', is no more a biographical remark than 'There was this Englishman, a Scotsman and an Irishman ...' is about three historical individuals. Similarly, the book of Jonah is not a blow-by-blow account of what happened to a historical figure: rather it is an adventure story told in such a way as to highlight the power of God and the narrow-mindedness of any prophet who underrates God's mercy and forgiveness.

One immediate consequence of such misunderstandings is to be seen in the hidden assumptions which underlie the often heard question, 'Do you believe that what the Bible says is true?' The questioner and the person who tries to reply often both share the same misapprehension as to what it is that the Bible 'says', because both have totally misunderstood the speech act which is being performed. The book of Job is not saying or teaching or assuming that there was such a person, nor is the book of Jonah saying that there are sea monsters capable of giving temporary hospitality to endangered prophets. Even to think of going to search for such beasts – which some fundamentalists have in fact done – shows that the book has been radically misunderstood. In contrast, people who claim to have seen the Loch Ness monster really are making a straightforward factual claim, which might be true or might be false even if someone thinks it absurd. But the book of Jonah is doing no such thing. Rather than ask whether a true believer has to believe in unlikely sea monsters and the mass conversion of a pagan city, one might well ask whether the believer accepts what the book really is 'doing': it is trying to convey dramatically that sometimes God's call to an individual may be insistent and in the end unavoidable, no matter how hard someone tries to run away from it; and that sometimes, sadly, even a minister of religion would prefer to rejoice in a God who punishes rather than in a God who forgives. The words of Jonah convey important truths about those topics; but they do not do so by narrating actual events.

How do these two examples relate to questions about translation? We can in this context assume that at least the book of Jonah poses relatively few problems when it comes to rendering its sentences into English. The same certainly cannot be said of Job, which poses very serious difficulties even at the verbal level. But the crucial point upon which I wish to focus here is that, even if the appropriate verbal equivalents can be established, so that sentence by sentence what is in the original is accurately, even if differently, conveyed by the translation, to read either of these two books as straight historical narrative is simply to misunderstand them. The people for whom those texts were written would have had little difficulty in recognising what kind of books they were, in the same way as a contemporary British reader would immediately recognise that *Animal Farm* is a political satire which intends to convey some important truths about totalitarian regimes – their genesis, their corruption, their effect on the simple and innocent citizen. It is not a wild account of some amazingly evolved super-pigs, an account which nobody would believe for a moment. *Animal Farm* is saying no such thing; it uses allegory and satire to say something quite different. So it is worth reflecting on how one would answer the question, 'Do you believe what *Animal Farm* says?', and what a sensible person might mean by saying that they certainly do believe it. Similarly, 'Are you convinced by Job?' is not asking for a response to a historical figure, but for one's assessment of a long and complex argument purporting to show that it is useless for mere humans to try to show exactly how God is justified in creating a world like ours. Some fundamentalists, however, even in these relatively uncontroversial cases, will persist in completely mis-reading these texts because they detect in the whole approach a critical attitude to biblical texts which they regard as dangerous in the extreme, even if sometimes it proves relatively innocuous, as it surely does in these two examples.

Other examples are indeed much more emotive, because they are seen as much more threatening to central Christian beliefs. I shall consider two groups of such texts: first the preliminary chapters and then the resurrection narratives in the Gospels of Matthew, Luke and John.

The infancy narratives

A recent BBC survey 'discovered' that 40 per cent of practising Christians 'did not believe the Gospel accounts of the birth of Jesus', but it totally failed to make clear precisely what the inter-viewers and their respondents took these accounts to be *saying*. A similarly naive questionnaire would probably have 'discovered' that nobody at all believes what Orwell was saying in *Animal Farm* about pigs talking and organising themselves into a political force. We can surely do better than encourage that kind of confusion.

There are no infancy narratives in the Gospel of Mark, which starts off at a brisk pace: it states that it is 'good news'; it describes Jesus as 'the Son of God'; it cites a passage of Isaiah which it applies to John the Baptist as the messenger preparing the way of the Lord; and, in verse 9, the adult Jesus makes his entrance. All of this in ten lines. The introduction to the Gospel thus briefly sets the scene for Mark's account of the ministry, passion, death and resurrection of Jesus of Nazareth. The reader knows from the start

what the point of the biography is; it presupposes a Jewish religious background of interpretation; its aim is to exhibit the ministry of Jesus in such a way as to help the reader to understand his
profound religious importance; and it makes a claim about Jesus'
status. So the reader comes to the narrative interpretatively
equipped, so to speak. A gospel, then, – and Mark's is the first
example of that particular genre – is not just any ordinary biography. It is an account of only a very small part of Jesus' life, the two
or three years of ministry leading up to his death; and it was written
to help believers to explain to themselves how it could be that a
Messiah could die, and what it means to be that Messiah's disciple.

Brief as it is, this programmatic introduction to Mark reveals
two important features common to all the early Christian writings:
the first is the claim that Jesus has a unique status; and the second is
the effort to reconcile this with the expectations of Jewish tradition
about the Messiah. Very much later, the Gospel of John will deal
with the same two issues, though it will do so in very different
language: the account of who Jesus was is much more metaphysical in style; Jesus is the Word, God with the Father from the
beginning, who reveals the glory of the Father in our world; but the
reference back to Jewish expectations is also there in the Gospel of
John, as it is in Mark. And, as in Mark, when the stage has been set
by John the Baptist, Jesus enters without more ado, in verse 29.

The Gospels of Matthew and Luke were written before John, but
later than the Gospel of Mark, with which their authors were
familiar and from whom they picked up some good ideas. So
Matthew and Luke, too, provide interpretative introductions which
set out to deal with very similar issues; but their idea was to do this
not by simple assertion plus a brief reference to the Jewish Bible, as
in Mark, nor by an elaborated, though still comparatively brief,
metaphysical account as would later be found in John. Instead both
Matthew and Luke offer an extended dramatic narrative, in the
process providing us with the vivid and memorable images which
give such beauty to every Christmas. Just the impact they would
have wished for.

Matthew begins with a family tree for Jesus. Its main point is to
present him as a descendant of David, since it was to David that the
messianic promises had been made. Its structure consists of three

groups of fourteen generations.[6] At any rate, some names are clearly left out of the list, presumably to keep to the symmetry of the fourteen: and despite the earthly family tree, Jesus' origin is from the Holy Spirit. It may be that the four women mentioned are included because they are Gentiles, not Jews, since Matthew's Gospel quite generally is at pains to point out that the message of Jesus is for all. To make just that point, the wise men come from the East and were led by a star – the Jews thought of the stars as angelic beings, emissaries of God. It is God himself who is leading Gentile sages to recognise the importance of the infant Jesus, while Jews such as Herod were set on rejecting him, just as the Pharisees of Matthew's time were hostile to the Christian Jewish communities for whom this Gospel was written.

Matthew then anticipates a theme to which he returns later in his Gospel; he has the infant Jesus, like the Jews of old, going into Egypt, an alien land: and the prophecy which Matthew quotes, 'Out of Egypt have I called my son', is fulfilled in Jesus, whom Matthew here presents as the new Moses, head of the New Israel,[7] led out of Egypt, and brought back to Nazareth; and it is from there that his public life is to begin. The theological scene has been set, just as Mark in his quite different way had set it at the start of his Gospel. Matthew's preface is much more elaborate than Mark's because he had the idea of presenting it dramatically, thus making it much more memorable. We hear of Jesus' origins, both Davidic and divine; we are led to think of him as a second Moses; and we are told that his message is for Gentiles as well as Jews. It is this theological background that Matthew offers us as a key to understanding his account of the ministry and death of Jesus.

It is surely clear that Matthew would have been quite baffled at the efforts of some of his nineteenth- and twentieth-century readers who try to identify some conjunction of the planets Mars and Venus to explain the very bright star which somehow moved to lead the Magi to Bethlehem, just as Orwell would have would have been completely bemused by any scientist who tried to investigate how

---

[6] The number 14 may be a kind of code, since the numbers of the three consonants in the Hebrew word 'David' add up to 14.
[7] Compare Matt. 2:15 and Hos. 11:1; and just as Moses is told to go back to the land of his birth (Exod. 4:19–20), Joseph is told by God in the same words to take Jesus back to Nazareth (Matt. 2:19).

the pigs in *Animal Farm* had managed to evolve speech. I suspect
Matthew would also have been baffled by their efforts to discover
any contemporary evidence for the massacre of the innocents, or
their failure to see how odd it would have been for a man, a woman
who had just given birth, and an infant to try to escape Herod's
soldiers by undertaking a long and difficult journey into Egypt.
Matthew would wonder how on earth we could have so missed the
point of what he was trying to say.

The account of the infancy and childhood of Jesus in Luke
provides an even more elaborate theological preface than the one
we have seen in Matthew. Commentators have long noticed the
way in which Luke's preface is written in a style which is a
deliberate throwback to the words and phrases of the Greek translation of the Jewish Bible, an older style quite different from
Luke's own 'contemporary' Greek in the rest of his Gospel and
Acts. The entire infancy narrative in Luke is extremely carefully
and formally constructed. We have two annunciations – one to the
priest Zechariah promising the astonishing birth of the future John
the Baptist to the elderly Elizabeth, and one, even more astonishing, to Mary, betrothed to Joseph, promising the birth of Jesus. To
each of them an angel – symbol for the presence of God himself –
appears; each of them is astonished and frightened; each asks for
proof, and is given an explanation of the unique ways in which
their two children will be called by God.

If, as seems possible, there was some rivalry between the disciples of John the Baptist and those of Jesus in later years closer to
the time in which the Gospel of Luke was written, these passages,
together with the lovely account of the visit of Mary to Elizabeth
and the interaction of their two unborn children, was probably
intended to emphasise the way in which Jesus and John should be
seen not as competitors but as having roles which were comple-
mentary. Their births are described in similar terms; and where
Zechariah praises God for John, the angels praise God for Jesus.

Luke hints at many aspects of the life and preaching of Jesus
which he especially wishes to highlight. Whereas the first visitors
to Jesus in Matthew are the wise men, in Luke they are the
shepherds – perhaps symbolising the poor and the unimportant;
and when Jesus is brought to the Temple, he is both the promised
saviour, a revelation to the Gentiles, and a sign which will be

contradicted. When Mary and Joseph lose touch with Jesus in his childhood, they too fail to understand the full truth about who he was and what he came to do. In Luke's two-volume work, the Gospel and the Acts of the Apostles, it is only after Pentecost that Mary and the apostles really understand the true significance of Jesus' ministry.

It is clear, then, that the purpose of the Lucan infancy narratives is theological and, as it were, programmatic. It introduces the whole of his elaborately constructed two-volume work, Luke–Acts. Luke's love of parallelism, which is so clear here in the infancy narratives, is characteristic also of Acts, in which the early Christians are presented as in a way reliving in their own lives and ministries the experience of Jesus. The apostles are overshadowed by the Spirit, as Mary was. The trial of Stephen is an especially clear example, in which Stephen echoes Jesus' own words; the deliverance of Peter from prison has overtones of Jesus' deliverance from the tomb; and the early preaching and healing ministry of Peter continues that of Jesus.

So much is uncontroversial. What is perhaps less clear is the extent to which Luke's infancy narratives might offer an account of some of the highlights among the actual events of Jesus' early years as well as being theologically programmatic. Luke begins his Gospel with a very formal sentence, in the most elegant classical style, addressing his reader and saying that, as many previous people have done, he too intends to write an 'orderly account of the events that have been fulfilled among us' so that his reader might know 'the truth concerning the things about which he has been instructed'. It might be argued, and some have indeed thought, that this makes it clear that Luke is writing what in modern terms would be a historical biography. This impression might be strengthened by the way in which after this formal introduction Luke proceeds to locate the coming of Jesus by reference to events in the secular world.[8]

---

[8] Luke 1:5–9 gives the dating of Zechariah's priesthood, Luke 2:1–4 the dating of the birth of Jesus, and the start of his ministry in 3:1–2. The dates are difficult to reconcile with one another and with what we know from other sources. Luke may have done his best to get them right, but in general have been more interested in making it repeatedly clear that Jesus' birth and ministry were for the Roman just as much as for the Jewish world.

But there are two reasons why one might doubt this interpretation. The first is the strange expression, 'which have been fulfilled among us'; this suggests that at least the focus of his writing is on the *religious import* of what Jesus did, which the early Christians for whom Luke was writing were themselves living out in their own way. It is to explain who Jesus was – a saviour and a man in whom was the fullness of God's Spirit – by showing how this shone through everything that Jesus did; and it also illuminates how the Christian communities of Luke's own time are fulfilling the purpose of Jesus' life. The second reason is obvious when one compares the infancy accounts in Luke and in Matthew. They overlap hardly at all. Even the explanation of why Jesus is at one time in Bethlehem and at another in Nazareth is different in the two accounts. Luke says nothing of a massacre of the innocent, a flight into Egypt, or the visit of the wise men; Matthew nothing about the shepherds, or the presentation of the infant Jesus in the Temple, or of his losing touch with his parents at the age of twelve during their pilgrimage to Jerusalem. It is surely not credible that each evangelist had discovered a series of historical events of Jesus' infancy which at no point overlapped with the events discovered by the other. On the other hand, when one considers the theology behind both accounts, one is at once aware of similar concerns evidenced in the points the two writers wish in their different ways to highlight, before their readers embark on reading what Jesus said and did during his ministry. Both writers emphasise his divine origin; both stress his mission as saviour, Matthew by painting him as a second Moses leading his people out of slavery, and Luke by writing the canticle of Zachary and the prophecies of Simeon and Anna. The massacre of the innocents in Matthew has the same theological function as the grim warning of Anna in Luke: true discipleship will be costly.

Fundamentalists, and perhaps others as well who would not think of themselves as fundamentalists at all, might feel rather dismayed at the general line I have just taken about the literary genre of these infancy narratives. John Barton, one of the foremost contemporary biblical scholars, addresses this kind of dismay in a profoundly important paragraph in his recent book on interpreting the Bible:

To anyone uninitiated in the jargon of biblical studies, biblical criticism sounds like an attack on the Bible. There has been a persistent tendency among those who are initiated to think that this is not so far from the truth. The contention may be that any critical approach to the Bible must reflect an underlying hostility to the Bible, or perhaps to the religions (Judaism and Christianity) whose Scripture it is. Or it may be, more subtly, that biblical critics damage the Bible even when their intentions are not hostile. A common complaint is that the critics 'have taken the Bible away from the church, and that some means needs to be found of reconnecting them.'[9]

'Criticism' sometimes does have negative overtones, it has to be said. And it is true that some biblical 'critics' did rather delight in showing that the Bible was historically inaccurate in all kinds of ways: there was no worldwide flood, no whale-swallowing Jonah, no parting of the Red Sea; the Gospels attribute to Jesus things he could not possibly have said; and so on. Whether these criticisms are made in a hostile tone of voice, or are simple factual statements, the impression given is that an important set of documents are being gradually shown to be worthless. The Dawkinses of this world have made their point, and there's an end to it.

As Barton goes on to point out, this attitude of dismay and hostility to biblical scholarship, in which Christians have unwittingly colluded, is based upon a misunderstanding of the texts. Consider the following set of contrasts:

The list on the left summarises the various elements in the infancy narratives of Matthew and Luke. There are comparatively few problems in translating the Greek sentences into English. But the import of the two texts is radically misunderstood unless it is realised that they are part of a dramatic presentation to introduce the reader to the true significance of Jesus' ministry, suffering and death. It is crucially important to recognise what the evangelists Matthew and Luke were *doing,* which speech acts they were performing, in writing as they did. If believers are to be interrogated about what they have to believe in order to be faithful to the

---

[9]   *The Nature of Biblical Criticism* (Louisville KY: Westminster John Knox Press, 2007). John Barton is Oriel and Laing Professor of the Interpretation of Holy Scripture, at the University of Oxford. The passage cited is on p. 137.

scriptural message, the answer is in terms of the theological truths on the right; for those are the statements which these two Gospel prefaces are making about Jesus. It is through these dramatic narratives that the two evangelists, each in his own way, endeavour to teach deep religious truths.

Dramatic narrative	Theological truth
Mary had a conversation with an angel.	Mary was a willing disciple, gradually learning the mystery of who her son was.
Mary was overshadowed by the Holy Spirit.	Mary's son was not just an ordinary Jewish child; he was a Son of God, his origin was divine.
John the Baptist recognised Jesus and leapt for joy.	There is no competition between Jesus and John the Baptist. They had different roles, indeed, but shared in the same divine call.
The infant Jesus was visited by shepherds.	The Gospel is to be preached to the poor, who accept it with joy and generosity.
The infant Jesus was visited by Gentile sages.	The Gospel is offered to all peoples, and they are ready and willing to listen to it.
There was a massacre of the innocents.	Fidelity to the Gospel will often involve suffering, even martyrdom.
Simeon and Anna prophesied sorrow for Mary	And this is a truth we all have to learn, gradually.
Jesus fled to Egypt, and returned to Nazareth.	Jesus can be seen as a second Moses, a Saviour leading his people out of slavery.
The young Jesus was lost and then found in the Temple.	All the disciples, even Jesus' own parents, even pious Jewish theologians, have to learn slowly the import of who Jesus was, and what it was he came to do.

Perhaps part of the problem is that people have been led to believe that the infancy narratives are straightforward factual accounts which aim above all to provide the *evidence* for the statements in the right-hand column. Hence, if these accounts are said to be imaginative dramatisations rather than historical facts, it might seem that evidence vital for belief has been thrown out. But the

New Testament as a whole makes it abundantly clear that the evidence for Christian belief about Jesus is to be found in his ministry – words and actions – and, above all, in his resurrection, rather than in his infancy. The point of the infancy narratives is to function as a kind of scene-setting for the reader who is preparing to read what the Gospels have to say about Jesus' ministry. Their function is explanatory, not an attempt to provide a justification.

One is tempted to say that we, as a culture, have rather lost touch with dramatised imagery as a means of conveying truth, as if truth resided only in the language of the physical sciences. Yet, after all, even to say that is something of an oversimplification. Firstly because the language of the physical sciences is itself often irreducibly metaphorical in the way it uses images to convey truths which outstrip our normal perceptual vocabulary. 'Black holes', 'strings vibrating in ten dimensions', 'curved space' and 'Big Bang' are all expressions which speak to us imaginatively, and which cannot without loss be reduced to the literal language suitable for describing the middle-sized earthly hardware to which our use of language is primarily adapted. So we can and are at times forced to use metaphor and imagery, especially at the deepest levels of contemporary science. Again, we can and do use film to suggest to our imaginations truths which go beyond the incidents displayed on the screen and for which we cannot easily find adequate words.

Twenty-first-century Gentiles, such as many of us are, may indeed not respond with Jewish enthusiasm to the image of Jesus as a second Moses. Matthew's Gospel was not written with us in mind. But what is important is that in a non-verbal way the imagery of Christmas does still *appeal*. The beauty and vulnerability of a new-born child will strike anyone, in any culture, and rightly remains central to our picture of Christmas. We ourselves have also elaborated the other biblical images in ways which appeal to us and do not occur in the Bible at all; so we have Jesus born amid the winter snow, since we know that his life is not destined to be an easy one; the shepherds offering their lambs express the gratitude of the poor; a worshipful ox and ass are symbols of a whole world redeemed; and the wise men from the East have become kings, so that we can contrast the simplicity of it all with a pageantry befitting a child who is God. But, also in contrast to the kings, we have our own ways of expressing the universality of the salvation promised by that child – our cribs are often ringed by people of all colours and nations; we sometimes have those notorious dark satanic mills in the background – our version of the slavery from which Moses freed the Israelites in Egypt. The designers of our cribs do not believe there were smoking factories in Bethlehem; but they have understood and refashioned – translated – the infancy narratives for our culture far better than many a literalist theologian.

In such ways we have tried to translate the biblical images so that they convey to our modern world the same truths which the two evangelists tried to communicate to their readers. I have already argued that the best translations often have to use different words and sometimes quite different images in order to speak to very different people just as effectively as the originals spoke to their original readership. The fundamentalist refuses to see this, for fear of losing what the divinely inspired originals contained. But any effective translation is going to have to say both less and more than the original. Not only the original words – in Aramaic, Hebrew or Greek – but often enough the original thought-patterns and images will have gone, lost in translation as they should be, just as the imagery of 'I am patting the lice' or 'The leg has no nose' has to go in the interest of communication. *Someone* has to have had the original imagery explained in order to understand it, just as biblical scholars have to try to understand the imagery of the texts they study, or else none of us will have any chance of understanding them. But, in order to communicate effectively to people in very different cultures what those texts are saying, it is obvious that new words, new images, new symbols have to be brought in. If this is done well, what is communicated will be both less, and more, than the original, but the truth will be essentially the same. Translation is literally an art, not a mechanical procedure. And perhaps I may offer what, for the moment, is no more than a passing thought: what of a younger generation, many of whom do not find that they are in touch with much of this except in a vaguely picturesque way? What will count as a faithful translation of the infancy narratives into their language? The crib, yes: and then what?

The resurrection narratives

I have suggested that the infancy narratives were not written in order to *prove* any theological doctrine, but rather to set the scene in such a way as to enable the reader to understand what was about to be narrated. I now suggest that the resurrection narratives, too, were not attempts to *prove* that Jesus was risen; they were intended to *explain* the precise significance of an event – in this case the resurrection of Jesus – which was taken as a given. A key point is that the resurrection narratives were written a good deal later than several other documents in the New Testament – later than the letters of Paul, for example; and probably later than the basic traditions describing the actions and teachings of Jesus which eventually formed the basis of the Gospels. The resurrection narratives were written to address the needs of second- or third-generation Christians, probably fifty years after the resurrection itself.

What, then, did the first Christians learn about the resurrection? There is a passage in which St Paul, writing to the Christians in Corinth, gives what is probably the earliest version we have of a Christian 'creed':

> *Now I would remind you, brethren, in what terms I preached the gospel which you received, and in which you stand ...*
> *For I delivered to you as of first importance what I also received, that Christ died for our sins in accordance with the scriptures, that he was buried, that he was raised on the third day in accordance with the scriptures, and that he appeared to Cephas, then to the twelve; then to more than five hundred brethren at one time, most of whom are still alive, though some have fallen asleep. Then he appeared to James, then to all the apostles. Last of all, as to one untimely born, he appeared also to me. (1 Cor. 15:3–8)*

Some twenty years after the death of Jesus, Paul wrote these words to the Christian community in Corinth, some of whom were inclined to reject belief in the resurrection. There are several quite striking things about it.

To begin with, it is clear that the faith of the early Christians was based upon the experience of a large number of people, most of whom are simply not known to us at all. Paul is careful to point out that some of those who first experienced the risen Christ were still alive when he was writing and, presumably, could be asked what that experience had been like. In contrast to Matthew and Luke, Paul here *is* trying to present the evidence in favour of saying that Jesus was risen, rather than explaining its significance.

Second, the repeated phrase 'in accordance with the scriptures' reflects what we know from elsewhere, that the early disciples had been profoundly shocked by the death of the man they had come to think of as the long-awaited Messiah. The Messiah was definitely not expected to die a shameful death at the hands of the Roman oppressors, if indeed he was supposed to die at all. The earliest Christians had to learn, almost desperately, to reread their Jewish tradition to find some pointers – 'the stone which the builders rejected' in the Psalms, and the 'Suffering Servant' in Isaiah, for example – which would help them to see that perhaps even such an apparent disaster could be somehow made sense of.[10] The first Christians had no hesitation in translating their Jewish heritage into Christian terms.

Third, it is quite remarkable how little correspondence there is between Paul's long and precise list of people to whom Christ appeared, and the resurrection narratives at the end of the three Gospels, Matthew, Luke and John. These narratives do mention appearances to the apostles – the 'eleven' in Matthew, 'the eleven and their companions' in Luke, the 'disciples' (twice) in John.[11] There is a passing mention of an appearance to Peter (in Luke). But there is no mention in the Gospels of a special appearance to James, let alone to the 'more than 500 at once'; and in the other direction, there is no mention in Paul's list of any appearance to the women or to Mary Magdalen, who are prominent in Matthew, Luke and John in different ways, nor of any appearance specifically in Galilee to correspond to the ones in Matthew and John. Again, the resurrection narratives differ greatly between themselves in ways which are reminiscent of the wide differences between the infancy narratives in Matthew and in Luke. And

---

[10] Ps. 118:22 was a favourite early Christian text, as was Isa. 53. The Messiah's death was perhaps, then, not altogether unexpected.

[11] It is not clear what Paul here takes the relation between 'the Twelve' and 'the apostles' to be, since he lists them separately. Could it be that he is here using 'apostle' in the more general sense which occurs in his letters, and is certainly wider than the Twelve? On this issue, see also below, pp. 136–40.

finally, just as Mark's Gospel, without any infancy narrative, begins with a single programmatic paragraph to introduce the ministry of Jesus, so it ends with an almost brutal abruptness, with the women staring apprehensively at the empty tomb having been told by two angelic figures that Jesus was risen and they were to tell Peter and the apostles to go back to Galilee. There is no account of any appearance of Jesus at all, though perhaps the experience of seeing an angelic figure in the empty tomb is intended to portray an experience of God which frightened the women without being clear to them.[12]

Here is a possible explanation of the differences between the four Gospels and between the Gospels and Paul. Paul talks about Christ appearing to those five hundred people and others as something which was simply common knowledge among the Christians of his time, without any need to elaborate on it; and the implication is that the experience of those people was not the common experience of all the Christians who, by Paul's time, had found faith in the risen Jesus. Paul did not mean simply that the people in his list had come to be consoled by the abiding value of the teachings of Jesus. He was no modern reductionist about the resurrection. To the people in his list, Jesus had *appeared.* To judge from the way Paul continues, it was not, or at least not directly, *that* point which was controversial; rather the problem was that some Corinthians found the whole creed very doubtful because they could not imagine what a risen person could possibly be like. Paul's starting point, then, the bedrock of his position, is the unquestionable list of witnesses. Only after reiterating that does he try to insist on the truth of the resurrection, and to make an effort to answer the precise question they were asking: what is a risen person *like*? I think it fair to say that he flounders more than a bit in trying to give any coherent answer.[13] In contrast, the resurrection narratives in the Gospels are, as we shall see, much more interested in *interpreting* the resurrection than in describing it.

---

[12] Some manuscripts have added some resurrection events to the end of Mark, perhaps finding it too abrupt. But the shortest version is what Mark himself wrote.

[13] In 1 Cor. 15:12–34 Paul insists on the truth of the resurrection of Jesus which is the basis of our belief that we too will rise: and in verses 35–58 he tries to suggest some ways of thinking about a risen body. N. T. Wright, in his admirable *The Resurrection of the Son of God* (London: SPCK, 2003), argues that Paul's account of resurrection conforms in many ways to the tenets of Second Temple theology.

Surprisingly, perhaps, despite the crowd of witnesses to whom Paul refers, we have almost no first-hand account of what it was like to 'see' the risen Jesus. Though Paul puts himself at the end of the list of people to whom Christ appeared, as if he were an afterthought, he does not give the impression that the appearance of Jesus to him was any different from his appearances to the others; and when he refers to it again in his letter to the Galatians (Gal. 1:13–15), he still gives no detailed description at all. The nearest thing to a description which we have are the two more detailed, but nonetheless second-hand, descriptions of Paul's experience on the road to Damascus given by Luke in the Acts of the Apostles.[14] Luke puts one of these into Paul's own mouth.[15] Three things are especially striking about these accounts:

1   Paul's own description does not suggest that in any ordinary sense he 'saw' the risen Jesus: that is to say, he did not have a vision of Jesus' risen body vividly before him. Yet he uses the same word when describing his own experience as he does for the experience of all the others. The word (*ôphthê*) is strictly a grammatical passive, and the most obvious translation would be 'Jesus *was seen by*'; the translation most common in English Bibles is 'Jesus *appeared to*', preferred perhaps because this is a bit closer to Paul's account of his own experience.
2   Paul had no doubt whatever about who it was he was dealing with, who had made such a dramatic impact on him. But he found that the experience 'blinded him'.
3   Paul's life was transformed by the experience.

Suppose, then, that these characteristics are typical of all the resurrection appearances mentioned in Paul's credal list, since he does not distinguish the appearance to himself from any of the others, except to say that it happened later. What, then, are the much later resurrection narratives in the Gospels trying to do?

---

[14]   It is likely, though not at all certain, that Luke was a personal companion to Paul during at least part of Paul's missionary journeys; the comparative restraint in Luke's account of Jesus appearing to Paul suggests that he is describing it more or less as Paul himself would have done.
[15]   Acts 22:1–16; see also 9:1–19.

The first Christians based their faith on the testimony of the whole host of witnesses mentioned by Paul, not on the resurrection narratives in the Gospels which had not as yet been written. The Gospels, written for Christians one or two generations later than Paul's audience, take Paul's list of witnesses for granted. Rather than rehearsing Paul's list yet again, their aim is to interpret those appearances of the risen Jesus, and to answer questions which those later Christians insisted upon asking, just as Paul's Corinthians did. The difference is that the writers of the Gospels could no longer easily refer these questioners to the first witnesses 'many of whom are still alive'. Many of them would by then be dead; and the audiences for whom Matthew, Luke and John wrote were scattered throughout the Mediterranean. So these evangelists too, in their quite different ways, give dramatised episodes, each of which vividly presents one or more of several different points, just as Matthew and Luke had done in their infancy narratives:

Dramatic narrative	**Theological truth**
Thomas is invited to feel the wounds in Jesus' hands and side. (John 20:24–29)	The risen Jesus is very definitely the *same* person as the one who died on the cross. Blessed are those who believe even though they have not 'seen'.
Jesus eats honeycomb and fish (of all things!). (Luke 24:36–43)	The risen Jesus is a human being, not some kind of disembodied spirit.
The disciples are sent back to 'Galilee of the Gentiles', from where it all started. (Mark 16:7–8; Matt. 28:16–20; as also John 21:1)	They disciples have to re-learn what it is to be a disciple, in order then to preach to the nations.
Peter and the others land an enormous catch of fish, and Peter is three times forgiven. (John 21:1–19; compare with Luke 5:1–11)	The mission of the early Church will be fruitful, and Peter's position of leadership is confirmed.
Jesus outlines the content of the mission on which he sends the apostles. (John 20:21–23)	The preaching of the early Christians is inspired by the risen Lord.
Jesus appears to Mary Magdalen in the garden (John 20:11–18). Unlike Thomas who had to touch in order to believe, Mary responds immediately to her name.	Our deep human relationships do survive death, however changed they somehow are; and our vocations are immediate and personal.

The resurrection narratives in the Gospels focus on the sense they made of their belief that Jesus was alive and on the significance of that fact, rather than trying to improve upon the description of the experience of the risen Jesus which Paul and others had. Once more, the truth is presented in dramatised and imaginative form, the more effectively to communicate it to second-generation Christians. Perhaps the most elaborate and ambitious of the resurrection narratives may serve as a commentary on them all. The story in Luke of the two disciples walking to Emmaus is a wonderful example of a dramatised narrative. To understand it properly, we have to think of second- or third-generation Christians, somewhat disappointed, asking, 'What is it in our lives which will parallel the experiences of those first disciples such as the ones on Paul's list? They were the lucky ones!' Luke's Emmaus story replies in three points:

1   There really is no need to find the death of Jesus shocking. Praying one's way through the Jewish Scriptures will gradually show you how God's plan in Jesus *was fulfilled*, despite what was done to him. The disciples in the Lucan story find this advice heart-warming, their despair relieved.
2   They recognised Jesus in the Eucharist: and that recognition went hand in hand with *not* 'seeing him'; for in that moment of recognition in the story, he disappeared from their eyes. This is of enormous symbolic importance.
3   Whereas – back in Jerusalem, now, for the dramatic scene has rapidly shifted – the apostles said, 'We have *seen* the Lord', the two Lucan disciples did *not* say that they had seen him too, as perhaps one might have expected; in contrast, they said that *they* 'had *recognised* him in the breaking of bread'.

The story is a kind of dramatised parable rather than the description of an actual event. Second-generation Christians have not 'seen' the Lord; instead, their way of experiencing his presence is to be through meditation on the Scriptures, and in celebrating the Eucharist. As the Gospel of John puts it, even to doubting Thomas, 'Blessed are those who have not *seen*, and have believed.' Not surprisingly, however, despite the enormous dramatic difference in presentation, the truths on which the resurrection narratives insist represent a much fuller and more focused understanding of those conveyed by the infancy narratives. The mysterious child is now shown to be a prophet, and more than a prophet, astonishingly vindicated by God. Jesus triumphantly fulfils the prophecy of Simeon. His coming transforms people's lives, providing them with an experience of the closeness of God, shining as 'a light for all nations and the glory of his people Israel'.

Part of the argument for not interpreting the resurrection narratives as straightforward historical descriptions is that the dramatic timing and settings are quite different in the three Gospels, with the result they really cannot be woven into a single stream of events; nor do they make any effort to duplicate or fit in with the basic list of appearances taken as foundational by Paul. So there is no need for us to give any thought to medieval questions such as 'Where exactly was Jesus between appearances?' The coin has another side, however. For there is a crucial fact which appears in all four Gospels and seems at least to be taken for granted in Paul's early creed. That fact is, of course, the empty tomb.

It seems to me that this perhaps is a straightforwardly historical claim. Paul's summary of the early creed makes explicit appeal to verifiable historical facts. All the Gospels describe the empty tomb in immediate relation to what was surely an everyday event, when the women disciples of Jesus went to anoint his body. Mark's Gospel, which has neither infancy narratives nor resurrection narratives, still describes the discovery of the empty tomb. Just as at the beginning of his Gospel Mark speaks of the Gospel as 'good news' and gives a single Old Testament passage as an interpretation, so here he provides a minimalist interpretation of the shocking fact that the body had gone. 'A young man dressed in a white robe', surely a symbol of the angelic presence of God, says straightforwardly that the tomb is indeed empty, that Jesus is indeed risen, and that the disciples are to go back to Galilee. There is no description of the risen Jesus, though the implication is that the women's experience was an extremely powerful and disorienting one which would transform their lives. The parallels with Paul's experience on the road to Damascus seem striking; for that too was a direct, almost indescribable experience, deeply troubling, which would transform his life. But not all at once: Paul represents himself as 'blinded', and Mark's Gospel ends with the simple statement that the women could not speak, so frightened were they. Similarly, in Luke and John, the discovery of the empty tomb is experienced as disturbing, frightening, life-changing, but it is separated from any of the narratives of resurrection appearances. This might well be a way of making it clear that the discovery by the women of the empty tomb was indeed something that did take place in an ordinary historical sense; and the dramatic narratives which follow that actual event are interpretations explaining what the implications of that historical discovery were.

As with the infancy narratives, fundamentalists attempt to understand all the resurrection narratives as straightforwardly historical accounts. In so doing, they create insuperable problems of chronology, of compatibility with the facts as made clear by Paul, and of inherent plausibility. In so doing, they run the risk either of forcing themselves to believe statements which are in themselves improbable, or of undermining their religious beliefs altogether. A position which is adopted as the safest way of being faithful to tradition proves in practice to be quite the reverse. It is not possible to be faithful to a tradition unless one has first understood what that tradition actually contains. In this instance, to do that requires a grasp of the literary genre of the resurrection narratives through which the truths they have to teach are conveyed, and in which one can then discern what the writers took to be the evidence for those truths. My attempts earlier in this section to 'spell out' the implications of the resurrection are rather crude and lacking in nuance, since I wished to state the essentials as crisply and briefly as possible. But, precisely because they are literal and lacking in imagery, the truths in my list are also impoverished by comparison with the vivid originals, which can stimulate us precisely because of their imaginative character. In the nature of the case, a resurrection experience is more difficult to convey than the birth of a child. For that reason, it seems to me, there are perhaps fewer modern equivalents to the resurrection narratives to parallel the way in which, as I have suggested, multicultural figures and dark satanic mills might convey something of the universal approach symbolised by the three wise men in the infancy narratives. But the principle is the same. To be faithful to a tradition, one has to hand it on successfully; and to succeed, one will have to speak to people who are very different from the original audience, whose cultural and intellectual assumptions, and whose patterns of imaginative thought are correspondingly also different. In this, the imaginative genius of the resurrection narratives has conveyed their theological message extremely effectively.

4

The Challenge of the Sciences

The birth of modern fundamentalism

Over the last four centuries, and arguably for longer even than that, Western civilisation has been characterised by the rapid development of the sciences. It seems that changes in the conclusions reached in physics, chemistry, biology, human psychology, medicine and sociology are occurring at an ever-increasing speed. One of the best known philosophers of science, Thomas Kuhn, has advanced the view that in each of the sciences there has occurred one or more radical 'paradigm shifts'. The 'paradigm', the overall framework which scientists take for granted at any particular time, governs not merely their basic assumptions, but also and consequently their methods and the meanings they give to the very terms in which their scientific beliefs are formulated. Kuhn's suggestion is that the differences between paradigms are so radical that statements made within one system simply cannot be compared with those made in a quite different system. For example, in his opinion it is not simply that the Greeks believed that an atom could not be split whereas we believe that it can. Kuhn argues that the two beliefs, apparently contradictory, are in fact not contradictory at all since the word 'atom' is not being used to refer to the same thing in the two paradigms. We and the Greeks are simply at cross purposes.[1]

The import of this account would be that translation between paradigms is impossible. There just *are* no common terms, no common rules of evidence, no common standards of research to form the shared basis on which translation ultimately depends. However, there are good reasons to suppose that this account is altogether too radical: it underestimates the great changes which can be made to existing theories in the light of further evidence:

[1] T. S. Kuhn, *The Structure of Scientific Revolutions*, 1st edn (Chicago: University of Chicago Press, 1962).

and it overstates the discontinuity involved in 'paradigm shifts', the more 'revolutionary' periods of the development of the sciences. Kuhn is nonetheless right to point out that change in the scientific climate of a culture goes hand in hand with an enormous difference in the ways in which people in that culture think. Even at a popular level, there is a vague but influential picture of which questions are important, what is going to count as evidence, and what will and what will not fit in with our overall patterns of thought and living. Religious belief too must be capable of being expressed in the language of the culture if it is to be credible at all; and if it is to appear intellectually honest, religious believers must be able to deal with any challenges in a way which respects what is best in that culture.

This task is considerable. It is hardly surprising, then, that in times of rapid development in the sciences, religions often give the impression either of a rather desperate attempt to play 'catch-up', or else of making a completely unconvincing attempt to insulate themselves from the contemporary world altogether. The enormous cultural shifts both in the physical and human sciences and in the practice of philosophy have had profound effects upon theology and religious belief. The Aristotelian revolution in the West in the twelfth and thirteenth centuries, the rapid development of physics and astronomy in the seventeenth and eighteenth centuries, and especially the revolution in historical, linguistic, biblical, and archaeological studies in the nineteenth and twentieth centuries which came to be called 'Modernism' (sometimes with approval, but usually not), have in their different ways presented considerable challenges to believers in all religious traditions. The same is true of the enormous changes evident in contemporary medicine and social studies. Sad to say, believers of all religious traditions have all too often been panicked into a disastrous attempt to cling on to the thought-patterns of outmoded secular and scientific cultures, and have been hopelessly slow to see that fidelity to tradition through a faithful retranslation of traditional beliefs is both possible and necessary. What is required is not a nervous literalism, but careful thought based on a renewed process of evaluation of exactly what it is essential to preserve from our past, as well as of what is required of us by the modern world.

Physics, astrophysics and Galileo

The rediscovery of Aristotle in the West can be seen as the first challenge to religion stemming from secular science. Not, indeed, that Aristotle was a scientist in the modern sense, quite; but the very scope of his work included logic, biology, physics, metaphysics and a philosophical account of human beings quite generally – our perceptions, emotions, thoughts, bodies and souls, as well as literature, ethics, politics and theology. Aristotelianism represented a system of thought which had genuine claims to be all-embracing. Not only did it claim to deal with almost everything, it contained the most sophisticated views about what counted as proper arguments, proofs and fallacious reasoning. In short, it presented a world-view, backed up by a comprehensive account of knowledge and the search for truth. Obviously, religious believers, who are also in the business of offering a world-view and are engaged in the search for truth, had to decide how to react. Should they simply reject Aristotelianism on religious grounds: or should they seek to accommodate it (with modifications, perhaps) into their religious beliefs (also perhaps with modifications), or try to discredit it on some other – perhaps Platonist – grounds? The challenge of secular knowledge to religious belief was of course not entirely new, but this version of it was immensely more powerful. And although Aristotle's scientific views have now been largely superseded, the shape of the Religion v Science debate has not really changed much from the eleventh century to our own times.

The Roman Catholic Church eventually – at the end of the nineteenth century – endorsed the approach of Thomas Aquinas, in sharp contrast to the attitude of the church authorities in Paris during his lifetime and after his death. In broad terms, it has now endorsed the view that religion and the sciences ultimately cannot conflict: some suitable consensus has to be sought. But by the time it publicly stated that Aquinas's Aristotelianism was an excellent vehicle for helping to express Christian belief, Aristotelianism was itself scientifically out of date. Only comparatively recently have serious attempts been made to bridge the gap between what Aquinas actually said (as distinct from the crude versions often presented as his) and more contemporary approaches to philosophy.

Once again, translation is not impossible, by any means, but neither is it simple; and, as always, it has been proved over the centuries that the devil is in the detail.

Astrophysics, and discussions of the soul, as represented by Aristotle, had caused trouble for religious believers long before the celebrated case of Galileo. The books of the Jewish scholar Moshe ben Maimon (also known by the Latin version of his name, Maimonides) were denounced by some rabbis to the Catholic Inquisition (!), who were more than happy to burn them in 1234. In Christian Paris, in 1277, Aristotle's works were condemned by the Archbishop, as were the works of Thomas Aquinas and other 'radical Aristotelians' who had tried to integrate Aristotelian science with their Christian beliefs; the works of the great Muslim writer Ibn Rushd (or Averroes, as he was known in Latin) were prohibited throughout Christendom more a hundred years after his death, and burned by the Arab religious authorities in 1306.[2] The views of these scholars were rejected by their co-religionists because they tried to integrate a scientific and rationalist Aristotle with their own sacred texts and traditions. Aristotle's apparent willingness to accept that the world might have had no beginning was held to be in flat contradiction to the first words in the Bible, 'in the beginning'.[3] The fact that Aristotelians found it hard to see how a soul could properly function without a body had led some Aristotelians such as Pope John XXII to suggest that there cannot be any temporal gap in the next world between a person's death and the final resurrection, a time gap during which the soul would have had to exist separated from its body. The theologians of Paris held that this contradicted the text in the letter to the Hebrews, 'it is appointed for mortals to die once and after that the judgement'[4], and asserted that, contrary to what Aristotelians might say, the souls of the just could enjoy the vision of God immediately upon their death without having to await the resurrection of their bodies.

---

[2]   Ibn Rushd was a scholar whose interests, like those of Aristotle on whose works he wrote impressive commentaries, were extremely wide, and covered medicine as well as philosophy and theology. He taught for much of his life in Cordoba, but died in 1198 in exile in Marrakech.

[3]   Some twentieth-century astronomers adopted the 'steady state' theory of the universe in an attempt to avoid the need to postulate a God who brought the universe into being. Fred Hoyle finally accepted the futility of such a manoeuvre.

[4]   Heb. 9:27. The Pope was persuaded to disown his previous views in 1334, and did so formally in a decree which he issued in 1336.

So the efforts of Aristotelians, including the Pope's own views, were rejected by theologians on biblical grounds – grounds which were surely very shaky indeed – and attempts to translate Christian beliefs in ways which would harmonise with Aristotle were treated with the utmost suspicion. Muslims, Jews and Christians alike were asked to adopt rigidly fundamentalist attitudes to their revealed texts in what proved to be a vain and misguided attempt to stem the scientific tide.

By the middle of the fifteenth century the scientific culture of Europe had changed and was by now in a very broad sense Aristotelian, despite the in-fighting between Ockhamists and Scotists, nominalists and realists. It was against this background, as we shall see later, that the Council of Trent was to insist that eucharistic doctrine should be re-expressed by using a formula which some twentieth-century Catholic theologians take to be part of Catholic dogma. But first I would like to skip forward a century, to a time when the conflict between science and theology seemed absolutely clear. The language and methods of the secular sciences was already moving away from Aristotle, and the need for further dialogue with the theologians was becoming urgent.

It is against these earlier controversies, ancient and modern, that we must understand the notorious arguments surrounding Galileo in the first quarter of the seventeenth century. Once again, the issue turned upon the apparently clear statements in the Bible that the sun rises, moves across the heavens, and sets, and the insistence of theologians that no scientific investigations could possibly call these truths into question. Even a relatively open-minded theologian, the Jesuit Cardinal Robert Bellarmine, found it very difficult to see how Galileo's observations could be accommodated. On 12 April 1615 he wrote to the Carmelite provincial Paolo Foscarini, who had supported Galileo publicly by attempting to prove that the new theory was not opposed to Scripture. Bellarmine began by praising both Foscarini and Galileo for being sufficiently cautious not to claim that Galileo's assertions about the movement of the sun were true, restricting themselves to saying merely that the heliocentric theory fitted the observed facts more easily. Bellarmine went on:

> *Second. I say that, as you know, the Council [of Trent] prohibits expounding the Scriptures contrary to the common agreement of*

the holy Fathers. And if Your Reverence would read not only the Fathers but also the commentaries of modern writers on Genesis, Psalms, Ecclesiastes and Josue you would find that all agree in explaining literally (ad litteram) that the sun is in the heavens and moves swiftly around the earth, and that the earth is far from the heavens and stands immobile in the centre of the universe. Now consider whether in all prudence the Church could encourage giving to Scripture a sense contrary to the holy Fathers and all the Latin and Greek commentators. Nor may it be answered that this is not a matter of faith, for if it is not a matter of faith from the point of view of the subject matter, it is on the part of the ones who have spoken. It would be just as heretical to deny that Abraham had two sons and Jacob twelve, as it would be to deny the virgin birth of Christ, for both are declared by the Holy Ghost through the mouths of the prophets and apostles.

Third. I say that if there were a true demonstration that the sun was in the centre of the universe and the earth in the third sphere, and that the sun did not travel around the earth but the earth circled the sun, then it would be necessary to proceed with great caution in explaining the passages of Scripture which seemed contrary, and we would rather have to say that we did not understand them than to say that something was false which has been demonstrated. But I do not believe that there is any such demonstration; none has been shown to me. It is not the same thing to show that the appearances are saved by assuming that the sun really is in the centre and the earth in the heavens.

Bellarmine's efforts to be conciliatory are brave, well intentioned and in principle very forward-looking, but in the end they were doomed to failure. He begins by flirting with the notion that scientific truth – scientifically true conclusions being those which most economically account for the observed data – might be thought to be in a different realm from revealed truths. There are two problems with this approach.

The first is that it is not easy to see how one can coherently operate with two different realms of truth in the way that Bellarmine suggests. To say that a statement expresses a truth is to say that it matches the way the world is. Suppose, then, that it is true that the sun revolves round the earth. It is therefore false that the earth revolves round the sun. How, then, does the heliocentric view

match the observations so well – 'save the appearances' so successfully, as Aristotle and Bellarmine would have agreed – if the world
is not in fact like that? There is the theoretically possible answer
that there are in principle an indefinite number of theories which
can be satisfied by a finite number of observations, so the geocen-
tric theory could conceivably be one of them. But Bellarmine is
willing to concede that the heliocentric theory might account for
the observational data *better* than any other, so one might suppose
that he realised it was simpler than the many epicycles which had
to be postulated by the Ptolemaic alternatives. When theories each
account for the observed data, simplicity, if not the only reason for
preferring one theory to its competitors, is certainly one of the
strongest reasons for doing so. Galileo could well have pointed out
that his theory would readily account for the possibility that moons
might be discovered orbiting other planets as well as Earth and
Jupiter, and so be shown to have greater predictive power than
Ptolemy's. It is indeed true that scientific statements are subject to
varying degrees of approximation, and can be proposed with
varying degrees of certainty. But that is not a reason to suppose that
the sciences make no straightforward truth-claims when they
describe what the world is like.

What Bellarmine rightly sees is that once it is conceded that
science makes straightforward truth-claims, those claims cannot
conflict with any truth-claims made by the Bible. Most interestingly, he accepts the implication of what he takes to be the extreme
case: if a definitively established[5] scientific statement were apparently to be in conflict with Scripture, then one would have to
conclude that we had somehow misinterpreted Scripture. The
fundamentalist alternative would be to say that the sense of the
Bible is clear and its authority is absolute, so it must be the science
which is in error.

At least in principle there are two basic ways in which this
problem can be resolved. One can say either:

1   The Bible is not inerrant in all respects. Thus Vatican II
    stated that the Scriptures are inerrant *when they assert a
    truth relevant to our salvation*. The Bible does not set out to

---

[5]   Bellarmine here uses *demonstrare* in its full Aristotelian sense, I think; a demonstra-
      tion establishes causally necessary truths on the basis of equally necessary premises.

teach the details of ancient history, nor scientific theories about creation. The age of Methuselah, the date of the governorship of Quirinius in Syria, or the order in which creatures appeared in the universe, are not relevant to our salvation.

Or:

2   The Bible is inerrant in all, or at any rate all but the most trivial, details. Rather than any exercise of human rationality, it is the Bible that is authoritative. Any conflict with conclusions of scientists must therefore be resolved in favour of the clear word of God.

It seems to me that Bellarmine, rightly but very reluctantly, opts for the first of these, in that when it really does come to the crunch he is more willing to admit that one might have misunderstood the Bible than to deny a fully and scientifically established truth. In contrast, option (2) leaves little or no room for such misunderstanding. The relevant biblical texts, most fundamentalists assume, are perfectly easy to understand. Nonetheless, though Bellarmine is not fundamentalist enough to adopt (2) wholeheartedly, he plainly does underestimate the difficulties in understanding what biblical texts are asserting. It is *not* obvious that, in the stories of the patriarchs, assertions about the numbers of children Jacob had are part of a historical narrative; and even if they were, it is not clear whether such assertions would be part of what 'is taught for our salvation.' But Bellarmine relies upon the consensus of traditional interpretation. The fact that the Catholic Church has only very recently withdrawn its condemnation of Galileo shows that such confidence can be, and at least in this case clearly was, misplaced for many centuries.

Of course, the fundamentalist reply to such a line of argument is to insist that to give way like this to changes in scientific opinion paves the way to a total subjectivism, whereby the word of God is interpreted and reinterpreted in accordance with the fashion of the moment. I have earlier invoked the model of faithful translation to counter such an argument. The first requirement of faithful translation and interpretation is to find out enough about the culture and circumstances and linguistic conventions of the text one hopes to translate; and when one has gone as far as one can in so doing, one then tries to find contemporary words in which *that same point* can be made. That this is not a purely mechanical procedure is amply demonstrated by attempts by computers to translate anything more than the simplest literal statements. But to say that translation is a skill rather than a mechanical process is not to say that it is a 'subjective' matter in any pejorative sense; there are objective criteria for deciding whether a translation is excellent, or is as adequate as one is likely to get, or is seriously misleading, or whether the interpretation put upon the text betrays a total misunderstanding of the literary genre of the original. In the case of most ancient texts, sacred and secular, immense effort has been expended in doing just these things, with very considerable success – perhaps because those texts have usually been approached with a scholarly objectivity rather than, as is all too common in theology, with a specific doctrinal interest already in mind.

One might be forgiven for assuming that, having accepted that Galileo was right and most of the Christian Churches wrong about this and about the process of creation, at least the problems in relating astrophysics to theology might now be quietly laid aside. Such optimism might still be misplaced. For one cannot rule out the possibility of new evidence suggesting that we humans are not the only intelligent beings in God's universe. Would we still want to repeat the biblical remark that 'all things were created in Jesus Christ', since that might appear to take for granted that, since Jesus was a human being, creation has a totally human focus, when God's vision of creation might be much less restricted? Or would we perhaps prefer to say that the Word was with God and all things were made through the Word? And how different could any revelation of God to some distant planet be from the revelation of God to us, if we assume that it is still the one God who reveals himself to them and to us? Of course God reveals himself to us in human terms, what else? But how might God speak to other created intelligences? Indeed, can we possibly give coherent answers to such questions?[6] Or would we be prepared to say that there never

---

[6]   One might remark that the existence of such a revelation would certainly involve the uttermost of translation challenges! Yet some scientists hope that *any* intelligent beings must share some basic truths with us.

could be evidence for the existence of such beings, since there is no mention of them in the Bible? There may be 'more things in heaven and earth than are dreamt of in our philosophy' – or our theology, for that matter.

The age of the sciences: fundamentalist panic

The difficulties experienced by Christians of all denominations in the second half of the nineteenth century were caused by the conjunction of several different causes. Initially, advances in the relatively new science of geology had appeared to many theologians and many scientists to confirm what they took to be the teaching of Moses on such topics as the flood, the rescue of the animals by Noah, and the six days of creation. Minor adjustments to the understanding of the relevant biblical texts were often adopted without difficulty: the six days of creation were not 24-hour days; for 'to God one day is as a thousand years'. Archaeologists had discovered the fossil remains of species of animals which were no longer extant; so Noah clearly did not save *all* the species of animals, only those he could find and take with him in the ark. The strata and composition of the world's crust were complex, but could be interpreted in a way consistent with a combination of volcanic eruptions and the Flood. And so on.[7] It was still possible – just – to work on the assumption that science and the traditional interpretation of the Bible could mutually stimulate and corroborate one another.

But the problems were in fact more serious, and it soon became clear that the scale of threat that they posed was quite unprecedented and utterly disorienting. In the first place, they turned up in so many different fields – in astronomy, since archaeological discoveries necessitated a radical redating of the history of the planet and of its inhabitants; in history, as a result of the growing understanding of the civilisations of the ancient Near East from which the biblical texts mostly originated; and especially in the theory of evolution, which had enormous implications since it called in question the traditional understanding of the process of creation as, supposedly, it was outlined in Genesis. Genesis surely

---

[7]   See the fascinating details cited in Charles Coulston Gillespie, *Genesis and Geology* (New York: Harper, 1959).

explicitly taught that humans were created fully formed; they certainly did not *evolve*. And it was clear that there was apparently a further incompatibility between the Genesis narrative in which Adam and Eve were the first humans, and evidence suggesting that it is probably not the case that all humans have the same pair of common ancestors, let alone that such ancestors could possibly have existed in an idealised state of original justice in the Garden of Eden. Yet the doctrine of 'original sin' as traditionally expounded required that we all have the same pair of humans as our ancestors, since original sin is physically inherited; and that Adam and Eve started off in an earthly paradise. Moreover, the theory of evolution did not simply threaten theology and biblical interpretation; to some it seemed to imply the reduction of morality itself to little more than a rationalisation of the survival of the fittest. And it was psychologically disturbing to take the revolutionary step of thinking of one's ancestors as, to put it bluntly, apes.

Worse still, all these threats were based upon evidence whose existence it became progressively more difficult to deny, and the threatening interpretations of which seemed to be more and more convincing. In comparison, the old doctrinal quarrels between the Western and Eastern Churches, or among the Western Churches at the time of the Reformation, might seem almost parochial. For those disputes had taken place within mutually shared boundaries and, for all their importance, they had not called in question the entire basis of Christianity as it had been understood and taught for centuries. By the middle of the nineteenth century the threat posed by the explosion of the sciences was radical and unprecedented.

To this crisis the Christian Churches all reacted in basically similar ways. A broad spectrum of Anglicans in England and in the United States tried to develop more sophisticated, but in fact fundamentally flawed, theories of biblical inerrancy. The Catholic authorities ruthlessly crushed any attempt to discuss the theological questions which had been raised. Its response to 'Modernism' was one or another version of fundamentalism, in which the Roman authorities decreed what was and what was not said in the biblical texts, and what could and could not be said about their literary genres, as if such factual matters could be settled by decree.[8] What was allegedly the 'true' interpretation of those texts was used to bolster positions in the sciences and in biblical exegesis which, a century later, were widely acknowledged by all the main Christian Churches, including the Roman Catholic Church, to be utterly untenable. At the time, in the early years of the twentieth century, efforts to retranslate the great truths of Christianity in order to make them intelligible in a quite different scientific culture were made by a few, but for more than half a century these efforts were seen by many Churches as evidence of unfaithfulness rather than as pioneering attempts to deal with a crying need. Even as late as 1951, when Catholic attitudes to the Bible had been greatly improved by Pius XII's encyclical letter *Divino afflante Spiritu* of 1943, his encyclical *Humani Generis* was still insisting that there was a problem about our descent not coming from a single human couple, though it stopped just short of saying that the problem is insoluble. Most seriously of all, well into the middle of the twentieth century no Christian Church of any denomination had comfortably faced the ramifications of the question, 'Have we really been so wrong?', which was what most troubled Bellarmine. But that was precisely how the question presented itself, and how, in particular, it was pushed by non-believers, including some influential groups of philosophers who endeavoured to call the whole of Christianity in question because it was at odds with the progress of science. Very convincing they were, since in many Churches authorities insisted upon maintaining positions which were scientifically quite untenable.

'How could we all have been so wrong, and for so long?' was the way in which the question presented itself to critics and bemused believers alike. And once again, two strategies emerged:

1   To challenge the various modernist theories: about the Bible, about traditional teachings, about the relationships between faith and reason. Such theories are open to question on scientific grounds, are incompatible with clear biblical teaching about the creation of human beings, and threaten the moral dignity of human beings. 'Good' science, properly

<hr>

[8]   See the propositions condemned by the Holy Office in the decree *Lamentabili* of 1907, reinforced by the encyclical letter of Pius X, *Pascendi*, in 1910.

understood, does not contradict our religious beliefs; the threat comes from 'bad' science which leaps to conclusions beyond the evidence, or from 'bad' exegesis which pays insufficient attention to the whole weight of the Christian tradition of biblical interpretation which determines what the texts mean.

2 To try to show that there is no incompatibility between scientific theory and the biblical texts once we have properly understood the point that the various biblical texts are making. Over the centuries, believers have created unnecessary difficulties for themselves precisely because they have uncritically and mistakenly interpreted almost all prose biblical texts as straightforward records of events. The sciences have done us a service by forcing us to apply proper scholarship, historical and linguistic, to the understanding of the Bible as we would to any other ancient texts. Moreover, improved knowledge has surely made it clear that biblical traditions even in the New Testament were various, and developed over time. And indeed not all the beliefs which Christians would later come to hold are already there in the biblical texts.

It will be clear by now that I find the approach suggested in (1) to be a mistaken way to deal with what is a false problem; and the proposed solution therefore is both scientifically untenable, religiously damaging, and in any case unnecessary. The first two chapters of Genesis simply are not a record of how God went about the process of creating, a kind of divine log-book or diary. The first chapter is by way of being a monotheist manifesto. In many ancient accounts of the origins of the universe, the existence of evil in the world is accounted for by saying that there is at least one evil god involved in creation. In contrast, the first chapter of Genesis insists that there is just one God, and that every thing which that God produced was good. This point is hammered home by each line of the story. 'He saw that it was good.' The final compiler of Genesis uses what was originally a quite different creation narrative in what is now chapter 2 to explain many features of creation. The God-given harmony between the sexes, the unsuccessful search for immortality, the fact that humans can be led by temptation to disobey God, the fact that there is a general sense of disenchant-ment with our human condition, all these facts are acknowledged by being given a mythological explanation, and explained in terms of an alienation from the will of God. There is nothing whatever in either of these two narratives which is in any way incompatible with contemporary science, nor indeed is there anything in the one which contradicts the other; the questions being considered and explained are quite different in the two cases, and in both cases also quite different from those involved either in astrophysics or in the theory of evolution.[9] In a way, then, I am indeed saying that Christians have for centuries been wrong on many of these issues. But I think a fuller answer should be more nuanced.

It can be shown, by the employment of the normal techniques for interpreting a whole range of types of ancient texts, that most Christians have been in several ways mistaken in their views about what the Bible says, what it *asserts as true*.[10] But it might be more helpful to think about the implications of what we might now wish to say about the Bible. We can start by saying that the books of the Bible are religious documents, and that they are intended to convey religious truths.[11] In the same line we can go on to suggest that the first thing to be done with any biblical text, be it a sentence or a much longer passage, or even an entire book such as Job or Jonah or Ruth, is to try to discover what its religious point is. What the sciences can provide is a negative check, since something which can be shown to be false in one or other of the sciences, cannot be a religious truth – or any other kind of truth. Of course in principle the same test will work the other way round: what is clearly a religious truth could be used to refute any scientific claim to the contrary. So the issue is twofold: first, to determine whether any conflict between science and religion is real rather than merely apparent; and second, to judge which of the two conflicting claims

---

9   To what extent these chapters are unfair to women is a different issue, involving the cultural bias of ancient civilisations, but not directly a conflict between religion and science.

10   I say 'most' in order to exclude the writers and the originally intended readership of the Christian biblical texts. I take it one can at least in general assume that they understood their own texts because they were steeped in the linguistic and cultural conventions which those texts presupposed.

11   This is in general true, but there are borderline cases, such as the Song of Songs, which may or may not have been intended as a religious allegory for the loving relationship between a human being and God.

is the more securely established. As a generalisation, though, it seems it will usually be easier to assess the truth of a scientific claim than it will be to establish precisely what religious claim is being made and hence to see whether it is or is not compatible with some scientific truth.

There was very good scientific evidence for Galileo's heliocentric theory. Bellarmine accepted that the relevant biblical statements might not be religious truths at all, any more than that there was any religious importance in the statement that Abraham had precisely two sons, Isaac and Jacob; he accepted that the only reason one might claim that these were truths at all was that they appeared to be asserted in an inspired book; and in this respect he wished to say the same about the view that the sun revolved round the earth; it appeared to be a scientific assertion in an inspired book. To resolve the controversy, then, one has to assess the evidence for Galileo's theory against the reasons for accepting Bellarmine's theory of inspiration. I have outlined above in a very general way which are the religious truths which Genesis 1—2 is inculcating: they concern the goodness of the one God's creation and the attribution to human choice of the evils and hardships of the world as we know it. In these respects, there is no reason to suppose that the two creation narratives in Genesis say anything which is incompatible with any scientific belief. The issue concerning the compatibility of the doctrine of original sin with what can be scientifically established about the origins of the human race is more complex, but not a great deal more complex. There is no suggestion in Genesis 2 that all humans – Cain, for instance, or anyone else – sinned *because Adam did*; Genesis 2 is a myth whose purpose is to explain very many things – the pains of childbirth, the leglessness of snakes, sexual longing and sexual shame, the struggle to till the earth, the longing for paradise and immortality – and it does so by seeing all these things as a punishment for seeking immortality in a way which was contrary to God's command. Whatever one might think of the success of that explanation, neither in Romans 5 nor in 1 Corinthians 15 does Paul say anything about sin being physically inherited from one originally contaminated couple. Once again, there seems to be nothing here which would conflict with scientific views about the inheritance of genetic characteristics from mothers and fathers which make it well-nigh impossible for us all to have had one pair of common ancestors.

What we are invited to do is to re-express whatever we believe to be valuable in Paul's parallel between Adam and Jesus in the language and images of our time. I have already argued that the process of translation is not a mechanical one, least of all when we are trying to give a contemporary interpretation of what was previously expressed in symbolic and mythical terms. Truth has to be preserved, or we would not be translating at all; but as my proverb examples illustrate, a truth can, and on occasion if it is to be intelligible must, be expressed in terms of very different images and literary forms.

Throughout this period, fundamentalists objected to the very notion that narrative texts could be anything other than factual descriptions of events. Yet, as a generalisation about narrative texts in any culture, this is patently untrue; and if the real burden of that criticism is that unless they are straightforward factual descriptions they cannot serve to convey truths, that is also patently untrue. As the parables of Jesus or the book of Revelation themselves illustrate, it is not even true of the narrative passages in the Bible. Alternatively, the fundamentalist worry is that the very project of 'translating' the Bible in order to make it understood in a radically different culture such as our own leaves all too much room for subjective interpretation. But again, were this objection valid we would never be able genuinely to understand people in another culture nor any of their writings apart from those which involve no metaphor or imagery or literary device at all. Quite generally, good and accurate translation requires a great willingness to learn facts about other cultures, and to develop a genuine feel for patterns of life and expression which may turn out to be very different from our own. That complex learning process is a prerequisite for accurate translation, but it is definitely not a licence to make it up as one goes along.

On the contrary, a good case can be made for saying that the impact of the rapidly developing physical and human sciences in the last one hundred and fifty years has been a great stimulus to a more accurate understanding of the biblical texts rather than a threat to the truths that those texts wish to communicate. In the process, it has highlighted the fact that the allegedly irreducible conflict between science and religion, dogmatically proclaimed by extremists on both sides, itself presupposes a mistaken analysis of the situation.

5

Shifts in Philosophical Vocabulary

Was Jesus of Nazareth a human person?

Translation issues bothered Christians long before our own times. There was a set of crucially important theological terms in Greek and Latin which caused endless confusion between Christians in . the Greek-speaking East and in the Latin-speaking West; and which often enough made it hard for them to agree about which views were heretical and which were perfectly orthodox. One such term was the Greek word *hypostasis*, which might, or again might not, be best translated into English as 'person', and which was a key term at the Council of Chalcedon in 451 when that Council tried to determine how we should think of Jesus Christ. Should we, in our own day and in English, say that Jesus Christ was or that he was not a human person?

Before we approach that issue directly, it is essential, for the reasons I have just given, to look at and try to gain an accurate understanding of the tradition to which the Council of Chalcedon was trying to be faithful. The tradition developed gradually, and in a variety of different ways. What was common to them all, to begin with, was the extreme difficulty which any Jew would have had in saying that an individual human being was God. Of course, in Jewish tradition human beings had often claimed to speak with the authority of God – and people were well used to assessing whether someone was genuinely a prophet, or merely falsely claiming to be one. Of course the Jews awaited the coming of the Messiah, God's anointed one, who would inaugurate the triumphant final and enduring Kingdom in which God truly ruled his people and the nations. But the Messiah, however unique the Jews believed him to be, certainly was not thought of as God. So it was scandal enough – a real obstacle to faith – that someone who might have been the Messiah should have been executed in disgrace. To have said that the crucified so-called Messiah was God would not just have been scandalous, it would have been a total impossibility, not something it would have ever occurred to the first Christians, Jews as they were, to say.

We do not have first-hand evidence of what the very earliest Christians said about Jesus. What we do have is what Paul says is an early traditional belief, that 'Christ died for our sins, in accordance with the scriptures, that he was buried, and was raised on the third day in accordance with the scriptures'. There are two very striking things about Paul's statement. The first is the repeated insistence that what happened to Christ was 'in accordance with the scriptures'. In so saying, Paul repeats a point which was central to all the early preaching, which attempted to show that even in Jewish tradition there were hints to be found about the death of the Messiah; perhaps, therefore, such a death, need not be totally shocking. The second is that in the early tradition the issue is not directly who Jesus was, but his function. They gave an answer to the question why Jesus should have died; it was that his death was a Passover offering to God. His obedience was our deliverance.

Our other source for the beliefs of the earliest Christians is Luke's Acts of the Apostles. Of course Luke's Gospel, together with its sequel, the Acts of the Apostles, was written many years later, and his account in the earlier chapters of Acts of the way in which the very first Christians preached is certainly in some ways idealised. It has been suggested, for instance, that in the early chapters of Acts Luke is giving his own view of how the Christians of his own day should preach to Jews: and when he tells the readers about Paul in the Areopagus at Athens, he is offering a model of how they might preach to Gentiles. This may well be so, but it is also likely that Luke would base his suggestions to a considerable extent on what the preachers in earlier years had in fact done. So Acts may well give us a reasonably unadorned picture of what those early Christian preachers said and the criticisms to which they tried to respond. They claimed that, despite appearances, Jesus was the Messiah; that he was raised by God from the dead; that he would come again at 'the time of universal restoration'; and that through him we receive the Holy Spirit who gives the disciples power and wisdom. 'The stone rejected by the builders', as they were fond of quoting from their Jewish Scriptures, 'has become the

corner stone.'[1] Paul had no hesitation in translating Jewish terms
for a secular Greek audience, and described Jesus to the Athenians
as 'a man whom God has appointed to judge the world in right-
eousness'. That description contains no Jewish terms at all.[2] In
Paul's earliest letter, he describes Jesus as 'Lord', which was his
favourite way of designating Jesus. In using this term, Paul
ascribes to Jesus a divine status. A good way to understand the
Jewish usage which Paul here assumes is to think of the first verse
of Psalm 110, which the early Christians often quoted: 'The LORD
said to my Lord, sit at my right hand.' The first 'Lord' in this
sentence is the reverential Jewish way of referring to God without
pronouncing his proper name, 'YHWH'; and the second occurrence
refers to the King whom God exalts. So describing Jesus as Lord is
a way of expressing the exalted status to which God has raised him.
Paul later says that Jesus was declared to be Son of God when God
raised him from the dead, and is the Son of God from heaven for
whom the Thessalonians are waiting.[3] He later says that believers
are said to live in Christ because of the gift of the Holy Spirit.
Nowhere in these early days was Jesus described as himself being,
without any qualification, God. He does have a divine status 'in the
form of God', as is said in a Christian hymn quoted by Paul:[4] and in
this hymn he is thought of as existing with God before his earthly
birth, a view which was also applied to the Messiah in some strands
of Palestinian Judaism. But there could be no question of thinking
that even such a divine figure was God, or in any way identical with
God. What Jesus did have, and what he was understood by the early
Christians to have claimed in his preaching to have, was a unique
relationship to God, a unique role in the coming messianic Kingdom, and an authority greater than that of any other prophet. This is
what Jesus meant by calling himself 'Son of Man', as his audiences
understood perfectly well, and which was shocking enough. But
when he said to his apostles that the Son of Man had to suffer and
be handed over they were totally disconcerted, for that was
nowhere in the original script.

[1] Ps. 118:22.
[2] 1 Cor. 15:3–4; Acts 3:11–26; 17:31.
[3] Rom. 1:4.
[4] Phil. 2:6–11.

Later, Paul came to describe Christ as 'the first born of all creation, for in him all things in heaven and earth were created',[5] comparing him to the Wisdom of God, who was, according to Jewish tradition, present at the very creation itself. The same Wisdom tradition lies behind the beginning of the Gospel of John which describes Jesus as the eternal Word of God.[6] Indeed, rather than starting with the earthly ministry of Jesus and seeing that culminate in his being exalted to the right hand of God, as the other Gospels do, the Fourth Gospel places the Word with God from the beginning, and says bluntly that the Word was God. His taking flesh and living among us was from the outset a revelation of God. The events of Jesus' ministry, death and resurrection are seen from God's point of view, and their inmost significance, often hidden from the people who misunderstand again and again, is revealed by showing that those events were signs, and by giving lengthy theological accounts of their deepest revelatory significance. The way was then open for the first tentative suggestions that Jesus simply *is* God, God become man. Yet even in the Fourth Gospel, this is still perhaps less than definitely asserted: Jesus says, 'The Father and I are one', which sounds clear enough: but even in this Gospel we read, 'The Father is greater than I', and, 'Believe in God, believe also in me', as though Jesus and God were somehow separate.[7]

Such was the earliest tradition spanning more than fifty years after Jesus' death. It caused later Christian writers to wrestle with real difficulties. The first, not often explicitly discussed, is that beliefs about Jesus had clearly changed and developed over those early years. The change was partly the result of grasping the full implications of the importance of the risen and exalted Messiah; and partly a consequence of Christianity moving into the wider Hellenistic environment in which it was at least possible to think of men, such as the Roman emperors, being revered as gods.[8] Not, of course, that the Christians abandoned their monotheism. But the very importance which they came to attach to Jesus meant that they

---

[5] 1 Thess. 1:10; Col. 1:15.
[6] Prov. 8:22–36. Wisd. 7:23–30 is in many ways echoed in John 1.
[7] John 10:30; 14:28; 14:1.
[8] Luke says that this happened to Paul and Barnabas themselves, identified with Hermes and Zeus by the people of Lystra (Acts 14:11–18).

had to think again about the implications of that faith for monotheism. Were Jesus and his Father *both* God? Both Gods? Fidelity to their tradition required them to make the effort to translate what their predecessors had said into the language of their own times and cultures; and it required them also to be faithful to the *process of thought* which was revealed in what their predecessors had written.

In particular, they found themselves faced with two interrelated dilemmas: how is the belief that Jesus was truly God compatible with there being just one God? On the other hand, if Jesus is truly God, how could he have been a real man? To neither of these questions did earlier tradition provide any clear answer, for the simple reason that the issues had never yet been posed in quite those terms. Unfortunately, that did not always prevent later theologians who took different sides of the argument from citing earlier texts as though those texts clearly took sides on just that question. In what was effectively a fundamentalist manner, both sides tended to assume that it was obvious which side of those questions the various texts took, and so they quoted from both the Jewish Bible (such as the texts from Proverbs mentioned above) and, with only somewhat more justification, from the New Testament writers, in an effort to give knock-down proof of their own positions. These texts were indeed concerned with the status of Jesus, but they certainly did not ask whether he was God (which in Jewish terms was quite unthinkable), or how his being God (if he was) affected whether he could be truly human. Earlier Christians had no intention of discussing *those* questions at all. It was simply obvious to everyone that he was an ordinary man, 'who was the carpenter, Mary's son', and whose brothers and sisters everybody knew.[9] It was his very ordinariness which had scandalised his early hearers when he presumed to start laying down the law; and when his disciples began to see that he was more than a prophet, that he was even the Messiah, they too were scandalised by his all-too-human death. What would any of these people, his hearers or his first disciples, have thought if they had been told that Jesus was truly God? Could they have taken that view as anything other than utterly pagan? Could they still have thought he was human like the

---

[9]   Mark 6:3.

rest of us? It seems clear that they would have thought the whole debate outrageous, and even blasphemous. Yet, those who knew of both the death and the resurrection of Jesus were faced with something quite extraordinary; they could no longer avoid being engaged in the debate which lasted for more than a century, like it or not.

Such was the complex tradition to which the Council of Nicaea, held in 325, tried to be faithful. They had somehow to get beyond the simple swapping of texts which had gone on for more than a hundred years, and, rather than simply citing them, try to *translate* them all into something which responded to the problems faced by their very different communities spread throughout the Mediterranean and Near-Eastern world, while yet remaining faithful to all that had been done and said. In the end, the Council insisted on just one key truth: that Jesus was truly God, one being with the Father, and not just in every way like the Father. The bishops at Nicaea were for the most part neither philosophers nor theologians. But they did translate. Their proposed translations involved metaphor (the Son is eternally *begotten by* the Father, but is not *created* by the Father; God from God is like *light from light*, spreading but not dividing) in the conviction that some mysteries are deeper than literal language can express. They did not try in any serious way to *explain* how this could be so, though it was explanations that some theologians on both sides wanted to hear and were ready to offer. So the disputes rumbled on, for more than another hundred years. There were one-sided views about Jesus the man: that he had a human body but not a human soul and certainly not a human mind and will, so that the only mind and will in Christ was the mind and will of God. There were suggestions that in Christ there were two natures, and therefore two minds, and two wills, with the consequent difficulty that to suppose that this kind of independence was present in one 'person' – whatever that might mean – seemed almost nonsensical. And exactly how are the persons in the Trinity both different from one another and yet one and the same God?

What the famous Council of Chalcedon did, or at least tried to do, in 451 was simply to reiterate that Nicaea had got it right. Jesus Christ was God from God, begotten not made, one with the Father; and Jesus Christ was also an individual human being, with a truly human mind and a human will, a man born of a woman who thereby was also mother of God. As they put it, he was

> One and the same Christ, Son, Lord, Only-begotten, made known in two natures which exist without confusion, without change, without division, without separation; the difference of natures in no way being removed by reason of the union, but rather, the properties of each being preserved, and both concurring into one prosôpon and one hypostasis.

Jesus Christ, in short, was one *hypostasis*, or one *prosôpon*, but two quite separate natures. But precisely at this point the problems of translation become really acute: how are we to translate those two Greek words? The table below shows some of the complications – 'shambles' would not be an exaggerated description – in the way in which the various terms were commonly used.

To begin with, there is a big difference between talking about human nature in general, and talking about the individual instance of human nature which is me: and, perhaps at first sight more strangely, there is a difference between talking about 'individual' as a *universal* term which can be applied in the same way to James and John and Mary and Ann, who are all alike in being individuals; and talking about the *particular* individual which is James, or the particular individual who is Mary. The same word can be used of each of them: but they obviously are not the same individual. That crucial ambiguity runs through both the Greek terms *hypostasis* and *ousia*. Think of the following confusing sentences, each of them true:

1   John is not the same *hypostasis* as Mary ('individual'; or 'person').
2   John's human nature (*ousia*) is not the same as Mary's (they are separate human beings).
3   John and Mary have the same nature (*ousia*; human nature in general).
4   You can use *hypostasis* to mean either 'individual person' or 'individual nature': and the same Latin word *substantia* can be used to translate either Greek word, both in its general sense, and in its individual sense.

The reader who finds that lacking in clarity can easily sympathise with the confusions and misunderstandings which resulted from the ways in which the same words were used in different senses by different theologians just before the Council of Chalcedon. It seemed almost impossible to determine whether they were agreeing with one another despite the fact that they seemed at times to be saying opposite things, or whether even if they could agree on a form of words they might still be understanding those words in quite different ways. Problems of translation seemed almost insoluble. As can be seen, there are no less than six possible translations in English corresponding to the single Greek word *hypostasis*; and the single English word 'nature' might be a translation of any of three very different Greek words. And note the tricky position of our word 'person' in this table, and the equally tricky ambiguity of both *prosôpon* and *hypostasis,* which could either be synonyms of *physis* and mean 'nature', or be contrasted with *physis* and mean 'person'.

Translation problems in speaking about Jesus Christ

Greek	Latin	English
hypostasis, or prosôpon	*substantia*	*substance(in general); a substance (individual)*
		nature in general (e.g. human nature) *an individual possessing such a nature*
		person
	persona	*person*
	suppositum	*subject, individual, agent*
		subject (of a sentence)
ousia	*substantia*	*substance (in general); a substance (individual)*
	essentia	*essence (definition); an essence (individual)*
		being; an individual being
	natura	*nature*
physis	*natura*	*nature*

So what was to be said about Jesus of Nazareth? The Council of Chalcedon said that the two separate *physeis* – the two natures, divine and human – came together, without being 'mixed' with one another, in the one *hypostasis* or (they added, trying to be helpful) the one *prosôpon*. Up to a point, that was perfectly clear: the one Jesus Christ is truly God, and equally truly a human being, and his being God does not get 'mixed up' with, does not interfere with, his being human. The trouble came when people tried to translate *hypostasis*: is the best Latin *persona* ('person') or *suppositum* ('individual', 'subject')? Suppose, for instance, we think of Jesus as an individual human, and the Word as the second person of the Trinity; and Jesus Christ as the name for the being in which both are united. How are we to describe Jesus Christ? He is one … but one *what*?

Suppose we try 'person'; so we say that there is just one person in Jesus Christ. But then it is natural enough to suppose that the one person is the second person of the Trinity (after all, *hypostasis* was indeed used in a different context to refer to each of the three who are united in the one *ousia* of the Triune God – as we might say, 'three persons in one God'). But the consequences of this can be disastrous. I recall a fellow student of theology asking, rhetorically, how it would go down were he to proclaim from the pulpit one Sunday that Jesus was certainly not a human person. For obviously, to deny in ordinary English that Jesus was a human person would naturally be taken to deny that Jesus was a fully human being, and hence to assert that he certainly was not a human being like us in everything but sin. Something which is not a human person just *cannot* be a fully human being. Worse still, theologians who nevertheless advocate translating *hypostasis* as 'person' often find themselves as a result saying that Jesus indeed was not a human person but a divine person. One mistake leads to another; it is easy to go on to suppose that his knowledge must therefore be far superior to ours; that he could not (not just 'never would') have sinned or be truly tempted, that he did not think like us, worry like us, become depressed or feel abandoned as we sometimes do. He was above all that – which surely suggests that he was not truly human after all. If pushed, holders of such a view might perhaps concede that the Word of God would *allow his humanity* – surely a very strange expression – to experience some limitations, of knowledge, perhaps, or power, or well-being; but this amounts to little more than saying that the Word allows himself to have some human characteristics and not others; and that is well short of orthodox Christianity, since it is contrary to Chalcedon's insistence that the two natures are not mixed up with one another *at all*. Scholars are generally agreed that the main aim of the Council was to insist that the one Jesus Christ was in the full sense God and in the full sense a human being.

So I suggest that it is better to say that Jesus Christ is 'one *subject,* or one *agent*',[10] who is both the second person of the Trinity and a human person. But how can two such different persons be a single moral agent, a single subject? The bishops at Chalcedon did not try to *explain* the mystery of the incarnation. That is indeed a mystery which is beyond our powers to explain. They were trying simply to insist on the key elements in the earlier tradition, as it had evolved, and to reconcile two or three sets of theologians who seemed to be at loggerheads. The Council refused to take only one part of that tradition in isolation – as if, for instance, the Fourth Gospel, presenting Jesus as all-knowing, one with the Father, somehow above the details of his suffering, passion and death, was denying that he was truly human, with limited knowledge or human feelings, fearful of what the future might bring. But equally they would not accept oversimplification in the opposite direction, as though the earliest Christians in order to be faithful to their Jewish roots were actually *denying* that Jesus could be God, rather than slowly coming to realise the full impact of who the man Jesus must also be. The Chalcedon bishops, accepting the whole sweep of Christian belief and practice over three hundred years, rejected both kinds of oversimplified answers.

By translating *hypostasis* as 'agent' or 'subject', we avoid the risks of suggesting either that he was not really God, or that he was not a human person like us in all things but sin. Jesus Christ is truly one 'subject'. So we can have sentences like 'Jesus Christ died on the cross' and 'Jesus Christ is one divine being with the Father', and have one and the same subject of both sentences. We can say that Jesus Christ is one agent, even though he operates on two

---

[10]   Using *suppositum* as the best Latin translation of *hypostasis* in this context, and taking *suppositum* very generally to mean 'subject' or 'agent'. Jesus Christ is truly one being, one moral agent, even though he operates on two quite different levels. I think this also fits *prosôpon* better, which is used for a character in a play, an actor. And 'actor' even in modern legal English can be synonymous with 'agent', the person doing something.

infinitely different levels. My preferred translation does nothing to *explain* how this can be; I would strongly urge that we should respect the tradition in which the bishops at both Nicaea and Chalcedon worked, by recognising that we should respect the mystery rather than try to make it disappear. This is not simply an evasion or cop-out. There is a good reason for not trying to be more precise, and it is this: God is simply not *literally* either one or three persons *in our sense* of those words; to use numbers like 'one' and 'three' literally would suggest boundaries and limitation: one thing is not the other thing. But God is in no way limited. Nor can one simply *add* God to Man, along the lines of the mythological centaur, which was man 'plus' horse. Those two earthly natures can be put side by side (or nose to tail) – because they are both earthly limited things. God is neither earthly nor limited nor in any literal sense divided in three. To say that Jesus Christ is truly human and truly divine 'without these two being mixed' is to recognise that there is an infinitely different, divine, dimension to the man Jesus, a dimension which passes our understanding precisely because it is not in any earthly sense a *second* dimension. To say that would be to reduce his divinity to something which could be counted on a par with his humanity. The Council of Chalcedon did not say that he was one *hypostasis* in two natures as though that *explained* anything at all. It was intent upon avoiding any kind of reductionism in either direction.

So what might it *be like* for a human being to be one with God? Perhaps the best place to look would be to think about the lives and experiences of the great mystics – who, as we know, had moments of the deepest consolation as well as feelings of utter spiritual abandonment. Their sense of union with God was, on their own admission, beyond human words to express adequately; it left their human experience at once transformed and yet unalterably human. Perhaps, then, all we can say is that the human experience of Jesus was at all times genuinely human experience – experience which any human being in principle could have – rather than what we might think of as experiences appropriate to a demigod. A demigod, some kind of *mixture* of human and divine, is precisely what Chalcedon says Jesus Christ was not. And, if we very properly have difficulties in speculating what it might be like for a human being to be God, we need to remember what is less often remarked upon, that we have at least as many difficulties in trying to say what it might be like for God to be a human being.

What has this to do with fundamentalism? I suspect that many Christians, from that time until the present, were well aware that *hypostasis* was the Greek term for each of the persons in the Blessed Trinity, and have thought that, to be faithful to the Council, the Latins must at all costs translate that word in every context as *persona*, and the English must therefore say 'person'. Anything vaguer, such as my *suppositum*, 'subject', would under-represent the tradition. Fundamentalists would be equally critical of my saying that Jesus, truly God and truly human, was nevertheless *one*, a *single agent*, as being too far from the original, and too weak an assertion. I would reply that the request for clarity in either direction is in the end reductionist and oversimplified.

The fundamentalist might simply give up, simply transliterate. But to insist in this way upon 'one word for one word' and 'staying as close to the original as possible', though tempting, is still a wholly mistaken account of what a faithful translation must do. On the contrary, as my proverbs illustrate and as is evident from this dispute, that kind of approach results in translations which can be simply unintelligible; witness the fact that in the catechism of my childhood we learnt the phrase 'the *hypostatic* union' to describe Jesus Christ, divine and human, as though that was a proper explanation, clear to us all, when it is neither. Nor, as far as we can gather, was it clear even to the Fathers at Chalcedon; but it was a very *useful* word to point to, rather than explain, an utter mystery.

Instead, we should try to be faithful to the approach we can find in the tradition itself. We try to learn from our earliest sources what it was that Jesus actually did, what he said, how he gradually saw that his prophetic mission was going to be less than the success he might have hoped; and we need to pick up which were the actions and events that led his first hearers to see that this ordinary man was a prophet and more than a prophet. We should, as they did, reflect on the resurrection and on what a huge difference the experience of the risen Jesus made to his first disciples. And finally we should learn from the practice of Nicaea and Chalcedon: it is essential *both* to respect fully the transcendent mystery of Jesus Christ, a thoroughly normal human being who is also the Word of God, *and* to avoid any one-sided oversimplifications. It is one and the same

Jesus Christ who is in the full sense a human person, and in the full sense God. That phrase, 'it is one and the same', is how *hypostasis* should be translated.

What exactly is transubstantiation?

There is a sentence in his first letter to the Corinthians in which Paul uses a slightly unusual form of expression. He says that the tradition he had received and hands on to his communities is that at the Eucharist they should '*proclaim* the death of Jesus until he comes' – proclaim as a joyful fact, in the same tone of voice as the early Christian hymn which Paul elsewhere quotes:

> *Being found in human form*
> *He humbled himself*
> *And became obedient to the point of death*
> *Even death on a cross.*
> *And that was why God also raised him on high,*
> *And gave him a name that is above every other name.[11]*

This 'proclamation' contains a very rich view of the value and point of Jesus, dead, buried and risen, and Paul wishes that the meal which the Church celebrated together should express this fact. He is engaged in criticising the Corinthians for discriminating against the poorer members even of their own community when they gather to 'eat the Lord's Supper'. He reminds them that in eating the bread and drinking the cup they should 'discern the body', since they live with the life of Jesus who is their food, and are 'answerable for the body and blood of the Lord'. 'To discern the body' is two things, then: first of all it is to recognise the underlying reality of the bread which is his body given to us; and Paul goes on to develop an account of the Christian community as the body of Christ, living with the very life of Christ himself since we have all 'drunk of the one Spirit'.[12] It is because the bread which is broken is the body of Jesus and the cup is the cup of his blood that the Christian community who share in that one bread and one cup are his body, and live with his life. To 'discern the body' involves

---

[11] The entire hymn is to be found in Phil. 2:6–11. It should be said, however, that not all scholars are convinced that it was once a separate hymn which Paul is here quoting.
[12] 1 Cor. 12:13.

recognising the profound unity of the Christian community, a community that confidently 'proclaims his death until he comes', a coming which they probably thought would not be long delayed.

The symbolism of the Passover meal which Jesus used at the Last Supper to explain the significance of what was about to happen to him is re-expressed among Paul's Gentile communities in words which speak of Jesus giving us his very life through the bread which is broken and the cup which is shared.

As is not infrequently the case with translation, the words being used are very different: the disciples at the Last Supper would not have spoken of themselves as sharing in the life of Jesus or becoming his body; and the Corinthian Christians would not perhaps have thought of the bread and wine as standing for Jesus, bleeding and broken, in the way that the Passover lamb in Jewish tradition perhaps stood for Isaac who obediently allowed himself to be bound, as God required, and sacrificed by Abraham; and who, when God provided a lamb to be sacrificed instead of him, thereby became the symbol of their liberation by God. The Jewish and Gentile Christians had perspectives which were very different. Above all there is the key fact that the Corinthians had, and the disciples at the Last Supper had not, learned to read the life and death of Jesus in terms of his rising from the dead.

Second-generation Christians might well have looked back with envy at the way in which the apostles, unlike themselves, had their faith confirmed by first-hand experience of the risen Jesus. There seemed to be nothing comparable to that in their own lives. Luke attempts to address this feeling by dramatising the problem in his story of the two disciples on the way to Emmaus.[13] This passage can plausibly be regarded as Luke's answer to a second-generation question about how his readers could share in an experience which could serve as a foundation for their faith, in the way in which 'seeing' the risen Jesus had grounded the faith of the very earliest believers and, later, of Paul. It is Luke's version of John's 'Blessed are those who have not seen and have believed'. In the Fourth Gospel, written much later again, the context in which the author places the Eucharist is not the Last Supper at all, but the feeding of the five thousand. The feeding is expressed in liturgical language –

[13]   See my fuller discussion above, pp. 54ff.

Jesus takes bread, breaks it and 'gives thanks'; but this time the symbolism is linked not to the Passover but to the life-giving manna in the desert, which in Jewish tradition was also a symbol of the people's obedience to God. As in Paul, the flesh and blood of Jesus is food which gives true life to those who 'come to' Jesus. Jesus himself lives in them. The phrases 'whoever eats this bread' and 'whoever eats me' are used equivalently.[14] As we can see, then, the eucharistic practice of the early Christians, from the apostles at the Last Supper to the communities of Paul, Luke and John, was embedded in significantly different cultures, and reflects different experiences of the life of the risen Jesus. Inevitably and rightly, the ways in which the Eucharist is understood, dramatised and expressed are, as one might expect, also very different.

Written perhaps at more or less the same time as the Fourth Gospel, the early Christian *Didache* gives us yet another way in which the experience of celebrating the Eucharist was translated, this time perhaps in Alexandria for a community of Christian Jews:

> *We thank thee, our Father, for the holy vine of David Thy servant, which You madest known to us through Jesus Thy Servant; to Thee be the glory for ever.*

Over the broken bread say:

> *We give you thanks, Father, for the life and the knowledge which you have revealed to us through Jesus your servant. To you be glory for ever. As this broken bread scattered on the mountains was gathered and became one, so too, may your Church be gathered together from the ends of the earth into your kingdom. For glory and power are yours through Jesus Christ for ever.'*
> *Do not let anyone eat or drink of your Eucharist except those who have been baptized in the name of the Lord. For the statement of the Lord applies here also:* Do not give to dogs what is holy.
> *When you finish the meal, offer thanks in this manner:*
>
> > *'We thank you, holy Father, for your name which you enshrined in our hearts. We thank you for the knowledge and faith and immortality which you revealed to us*

[14] John 6, and in particular verses 52–58.

> *through your servant Jesus. To you be glory for ever.*
> *Almighty ruler, you created all things for the sake of your*
> *name; you gave us food and drink to enjoy so that we*
> *might give you thanks. Now you have favoured us through*
> *Jesus your servant with spiritual food and drink as well as*
> *with eternal life. Above all we thank you because you are*
> *mighty. To you be glory for ever.'[15]*

To sum up: the considerable differences between the various ways in which the early Christians expressed their eucharistic faith seem to have been quite uncontroversial, and were readily seen as different formulations of the same practice adapted quite naturally to the history of the different communities.

Things were very different in the Middle Ages, and head-on controversies multiplied. The fundamental fact which most of the medieval theologians wished to insist upon was that the 'is' in 'This is my body' (and similarly for the blood) had to be understood literally; it was *not* the same as saying that the apple-paste at the Seder meal *is* (meaning 'represents') the mortar with which the Israelite slaves had to lay bricks for Pharaoh, or that the lamb eaten at Passover *symbolises* the body of Isaac. The bread and wine *became* the body and blood of Christ. The difficulty in so saying was clearly that there was no obvious change discernible, whether at the Last Supper, or in the Emmaus story, or in the Christian eucharistic meals. It was this gap between belief and appearances, a gap not seen as at all problematic in earlier centuries, which medieval speculation found so difficult to handle. Controversies abounded from the eleventh until the sixteenth century.

An early sign of the difficulties to come had already appeared in 1059, when Berengar, a canon of the cathedral of Tours, was required to swear that he believed,

> *... that after the consecration the bread and wine are not merely*
> *the sacrament, but also the true body and blood of our Lord*
> *Jesus Christ; and it is not just in the sacrament but in truth that*
> *the body of Christ is felt and broken by the hands of the priest,*
> *and crushed by the teeth of the faithful.*

---

[15] 'The Teaching of the twelve Apostles to the Gentiles', 9–10.

Berengar was plainly uncomfortable with the second half of what he had been asked to say, and, once he got home, soon reverted to what he took to be the more traditional use of the language of sacrament and symbol. As a result, some twenty years later, he was once more required to profess his faith under oath that,

> *After the consecration [the bread and wine] are the true body of Christ and the blood which flowed from his side, not just through the sign and power of the sacrament, but in the individuality of [their] nature and the truth of their substance.*

Between the controversy with Berengar and the Council of Trent, Western thought had been revolutionised, as we have already discussed, by the rediscovery of the works of Aristotle, whom they regarded as both a philosopher and a scientist, a student of nature. [16] Perhaps for the first time, the Western Church had to think seriously about the relationship between its theology and the sciences. Policies ranged from the outright rejection of Aristotle as incompatible with Christian tradition, to the attempts to re-express the truths of the faith in terms which harmonised with those of Aristotle. It was in this spirit that various schools of theology, using terminology adapted in different ways from Aristotle, tried to explain this 'sacrament' and 'sacramental presence' in terms of his theory of substance. The Council of Trent adopted this method in an attempt to clarify Catholic teaching at a time when various accounts of the Eucharist were being proposed by both Catholic and Protestant theologians. The aim was to say something which was entirely faithful to the tradition which went back to St Paul and the earliest Christians. Paul had written: 'The Lord Jesus ... said "This is my body that is for you: do this in remembrance of me." In the same way he took the cup also, after supper, saying "This cup is the new covenant in my blood" ' (1 Cor. 11:24–25). And John's Gospel was equally forthright: 'My flesh is true food, and my blood is true drink: those who eat my flesh and drink my blood abide in me and I in them' (John 6:55–56).

What looks like bread and wine is truly the body and blood of Christ. The Council wished to say that this was true independently

---

[16]   See above, pp. 60–1.

of whether or not a person believed it; and it further hoped to explain how it could be that the bread was more than a symbol of the body of Christ, since they took it that the biblical texts clearly meant more than that. 'Symbolise', they thought, was too weak an expression, and in any case the Council believed that the implication of that Pauline and several Johannine texts was that there was no longer any bread there to act as a symbol. The Council tried to put things positively, and to *explain how* what the Lord Jesus said can be true. In so doing it goes a great deal further than Paul or John could have done, because it attempts to re-express the biblical statements in the language of the best science of their time, by invoking the Aristotelian concepts of substance and accident. The desire that religion should take the progress of science seriously is surely admirable. The effort was well intentioned, but in this case of limited utility. As five centuries of subsequent discussion have made clear, the attempts to adapt Aristotle to what Christians had constantly practised not merely produced quite insoluble inconsistencies; it also failed to understand the fact that Aristotelian physics of substance and accident simply could not explain a practice which had nothing to do with physics at all – the proclamation of the death of Jesus until he should come again. The problem is not whether science and faith should talk to one another: of course they can, and so they should if religious beliefs are to be integrated with the rest of human life. But theology and the human sciences each have their limitations, as they both must recognise. The sciences need to accept that not everything in our world is accessible to the methods of chemistry or physics: and faith surely must recognise that to grasp anything of a transcendent God – a God who cannot be adequately captured in the words suitable for this-world realities – is to work at the very tenuous limits of the human mind. Clarity is not to be had, and attempts to tie everything up in neat scientific ribbons almost certainly will reduce a profound mystery to an everyday falsehood. Indeed, Aristotelian science was recognised to be simply inadequate for the task, as the Council itself explicitly says, 'Even if we can hardly express this way of existing in words, we state that it is still possible for God, and that we can go along with it with our thought illuminated by faith, and must constantly believe it.'[17]

Nothing daunted, however, the Council later seems to become more heedless of its own warnings about the inadequacy of words to express the mystery of faith:

> *Since Christ our Redeemer said that it was truly his own body which he was offering under the form of bread, there has therefore always been complete conviction in the Church of God ... that by the consecration of the bread and wine there takes place the change of the whole substance of the bread into the substance of the body of our Lord, and of the whole substance of the wine into the substance of his blood ... while the appearances of bread and wine remain, a change which the Catholic church most aptly and accurately calls transubstantiation.*

The Council also directs an anathema against anyone who denies that

> *In the sacrament of the most Holy Eucharist is contained the body and blood of Our Lord Jesus Christ, together with his soul and divinity, and hence the whole Christ, but says instead that it is therein contained only in sign, or figure, or effectiveness.*[18]

Or who denies that 'Christ in the Eucharist is eaten not merely spiritually but also sacramentally and really.'

What is at issue here? In the first place, have later Christians correctly understood what St Paul and the Fourth Gospel meant? Then, were the efforts to re-express that meaning in the language of

---

[17] The admission is in the decree on the Eucharist, ch. 1, Denzinger-Schönmetzer 1636. It is not hard to see the inadequacies. If someone were to ask what it is that looks white and tastes like bread, etc., the answer would have to be that nothing does that – those 'looks' and 'tastes' are not the look or taste of anything at all; if asked whether Christ's body as present in the Eucharist has its usual size and shape and all its other properties, the answer would have to be that of course it does, but that none of these is accessible to our senses. (See, for instance, Thomas Aquinas, *Summa Theologiae* III, q. 76, a. 4–7, and q. 77, a.1.) These claims are surely very strange, and in Aristotle's own terms almost unintelligible. Moreover, the Fathers at Trent themselves did not agree on what 'substance' meant. For a full account of the difficulties of eucharistic language, see P. J. Fitzpatrick, *In Breaking of Bread* (Cambridge: Cambridge University Press, 1993).

[18] The Latin texts can be found in DS 1642, 1651, 1658.

medieval science helpful? And finally, is the language of medieval science the best for *us* to use if we try to express the same beliefs in our own contemporary idiom?

It has to be said that the medieval terminology was not consistent, nor was it consistently used in official pronouncements. Berengar was forced to deny that Jesus was present merely 'in sacrament' as contrasted with 'in truth'; whereas Trent insisted that Jesus was present not merely in sign, figure and effectiveness, but also *sacramentally and in reality*. The words 'sacramentally' and 'really' are repeated, but in such a way that they cannot possibly have the same sense as in the earlier dispute. That the sacrament 'has the effect (or 'power') of Christ's body and blood' is held to be insufficiently realist, though one might have thought that to have a causal effect was as good a test as can be devised for being real; after all, mere symbols have no such effects. How, then, are we to translate 'sacramentally' or 'really' in order to be faithful to that tradition?

In our own day, the theologians who were members of ARCIC[19] held many discussions about the presence of Christ in the Eucharist, and finally reached agreement on what could be said. Their conclusions were couched in a combination of the language of the New Testament and ordinary contemporary English. In their final 'elucidation' they say:

> *His body and blood are given through the action of the Holy Spirit, appropriating bread and wine so that they become the food of the new creation already inaugurated by the coming of Christ.*
>
> *Becoming does not here imply material change. Nor does the liturgical use of the word imply that the bread and wine become Christ's body and blood in such a way that his presence is limited to the consecrated elements. It does not imply that Christ becomes present in the Eucharist in the same manner that he was present in his earthly life. It does not imply that this becoming follows the physical laws of this world. What is here affirmed is a sacramental presence in which God uses the realities of this world to convey the realities of the new creation:*

---

[19]   The Anglican–Roman Catholic International Commission, which was asked to consider whether the two Churches could agree on a common belief, in this case about the Eucharist. Their 'Final Report' was issued in 1981.

bread for this life becomes the bread of eternal life. Before the eucharistic prayer, to the question 'What is that?', the believer answers 'It is bread'. After the eucharistic prayer, to the same question he answers, 'It is truly the body of Christ, the Bread of Life'.

Compare that statement with the citations from Trent given above. The traditional sense is surely well preserved by the ARCIC version, which translates that truth into the plain language which we normally use, and which captures what the ordinary Christian would wish to say about the rite in which they participate. The language of Trent, whatever its merits in the context in which it was invoked, is in our culture obscure and potentially misleading. It is not that the Tridentine version of Christian tradition is *mistaken*, but one might well wonder whether that particular approach to formulating Catholic faith could ever really have succeeded: at any rate, it cannot be translated word for word into our twenty-first-century language without becoming unintelligible. The truths which Trent wished to insist upon against some of the Reformers (perhaps especially Zwingli) could have been put in plain speech perfectly adequately. All the more regrettable, then, is the grudging language of the *Catholic Response to ARCIC 1*:

The affirmations that the Eucharist is 'the Lord's real gift of himself to his Church' and that the bread and wine 'become' the body and blood of Christ can certainly be interpreted in conformity with Catholic faith. They are insufficient, however, to remove all ambiguity regarding the mode of the real presence which is due to a substantial change in the elements. The Catholic Church holds that Christ in the Eucharist makes himself present sacramentally and substantially when under the species of bread and wine these earthly realities are changed into the reality of his Body and Blood, Soul and Divinity.

What was understood by the term 'of one substance' at this time was believed to express the content of Christian faith concerning Christ, even though the actual term is never used in the apostolic writings. This combination of permanence in the revealed truth and continuous exploration of its meaning is what is meant by Christian tradition. Some of the results of this reflection, which bear upon essential matters of faith, have come

> *to be recognized as the authentic expression of Christian*
> *doctrine and therefore part of the 'deposit of faith'.*

I imagine that the theologians who were members of ARCIC thought that, rather than being a helpful explanation of the real presence of Christ in the Eucharist, the theory of transubstantiation is nowadays very hard to understand and potentially misleading. Whatever else, it certainly did not 'remove all ambiguity'. The ARCIC theologians did not believe that what is ultimately a mystery of faith can helpfully be expressed in scientific terms, let alone the terms of Aristotelian science. So ARCIC tried to say what is and is not the case in simple English, using words which relate to contemporary physics in the same kind of way that the words used by Trent related to Aristotle and his medieval interpreters. ARCIC avoids expressions such as 'Not merely spiritually, but sacramentally and really' because they are either misleading or almost unintelligible in today's English-speaking world. And, as I pointed out above, there is at least one place where Trent itself says that its words are hardly adequate.

Which more clearly expresses both what Christians can see with their own eyes and what Christians believe? The official Roman *Response* here has what is in essence a fundamentalist attitude to Trent, in that it assumes that *only* by transliterating the technical terms from another culture can one guarantee a translation which is faithful to the original. This particular translation, though not in the New Testament, is nevertheless said by some theologians to have become part of 'the deposit of faith'. Hardly; at most it might have been an acceptable way of formulating that belief in the technical language of the time, though it certainly generated some confusions even then. It clearly cannot be best for us – because in plain English it suggests the opposite of the truth. It is simply misleading to use 'species', 'elements' and 'substantially' as if these terms, so used, are clear to the contemporary English speaker, or as if they mean now what they meant in medieval philosophy. In contemporary English, 'species' means 'kind', often a biological kind, and has nothing to do with 'appearance', as this passage apparently intends; 'elements' in contemporary English refers to the basic chemicals of our world; what precisely it is meant to refer to in this passage is anybody's guess; and 'substance' and 'substantially' do not now mean what they meant at the Council of Nicaea at which the Son was said to be one *in being* with the Father.

This discussion of the Eucharist illustrates the way in which I have been arguing against an unnecessary, and in the end unhelpful, literalist approach to translation. From its inception, Christian tradition has been willing to re-express even its most basic beliefs in terms which were adapted to the various cultures in which Christian communities grew up. There are notable differences of imagery and language from Paul to Matthew, to John; and from the biblical writers to Aquinas; and from Aquinas to Trent. As with some of my proverb examples, a word-for-word translation can be an essential *part* of trying to understand what was meant, and can be helpful to bring home to us the practice of a very different culture. But when, as with 'I am patting the lice', or 'The leg has no nose', the word-for-word rendering is unintelligible to us, it is thereby inadequate as a translation. Any successful attempt to say what the common thread is or to identify 'the essence' of the tradition to which they all faithfully belong will inevitably say both *less and more* than is said in each of the other living expressions of that tradition. Contemporary Christians do not think of Isaac; and the disciples at the Last Supper or the early Christian Churches knew nothing of 'substance' and 'elements'. Why should they? Is there any good reason to say that their faith was thereby undeveloped by comparison with ours? Must we still talk in a language which was almost out of date at the time of Trent?

A nervous effort in the interests of fidelity simply to repeat what was once said in a totally different culture is doomed to failure; what is needed is a mutual reaching across a gap, a willingness to move as well as to connect. In this, the New Testament writers themselves have surely set us an example we should not be afraid to follow. They did not simply adopt one fixed terminology; they expressed what they were doing in the Eucharist in various ways, which the others could nonetheless recognise. There need not be just one way of expressing in words what they were doing together in proclaiming the death of the Lord until he comes; indeed such an overwhelming mystery is surely going to give rise to many human attempts to talk about it and bring it home to ourselves, while accepting that none of them can be a full explanation of *how* it all comes about.

6

Behaviour in Different Cultures

How do we know what someone is doing?

Consider the following statement in Matthew's Gospel:

> *Then Jesus said to the crowds and to his disciples: 'The scribes*
> *and Pharisees sit on Moses' seat; therefore do whatever they*
> *teach you and follow it; but do not do what they do, for they do*
> *not practise what they teach.'*[1]

Is there any way in which a Christian nowadays could take this
advice and follow it? Can one really speak of 'translating' actions
from one setting into another, from one culture into another? It
might seem that it hardly makes sense: translation, after all, is a
procedure which deals with words, not actions. Nonetheless, I
think it is worth pursuing the idea of translating actions from one
setting into another, just as one thinks of translating what someone
says from one language into another. There are enough indications
that the parallel ought to hold. Both words and actions are ways in
which we express ourselves: and both in the case of actions and of
words the meaning of what is done or said will vary according to
circumstances. Again, we have words which we use to describe
actions; and it would not be possible to translate action words from
one language into another were it not the case that the actions we
refer to when we use those words are in the relevant way truly
comparable. Moreover, one can think back to some of the ways in
which translations from one language to another can be less than
adequate. They can be slavishly word for word when that simply is
unhelpful or inappropriate. The follower of Jesus today going
round looking for some scribes and Pharisees to obey but not
imitate is making the same kind of mistake as the person who
thinks that 'God's child in the hatbox' is a suitable translation for

---

[1]   Matt. 23:2–3.

the German expression 'Das Kind Gottes in der Hutschachtel'. In a general way, practical advice, where it is to be followed at all, is to be followed *mutatis mutandis* – adapting it when necessary. So perhaps the translation model is not so useless after all. But neither, as we have seen, is it a simple matter to get it right.

The fuzziness of action words

The first complication arises because even when it seems reasonably clear how we should translate various words in other languages, in all probability the precise *application* of these terms is not going to be in every respect identical. It is by and large true to say that only in the case of totally abstract terms such as are used in mathematics or logic is the correct application of any word guaranteed to be quite precise. The real world is less clear. I may know that *fauteuil* in French means 'armchair'. But exactly what counts as an armchair and not just a chair with arms? Exactly what makes something a table rather than a desk? Should we say that this is a mat rather than a rug, or that it is raining rather than just drizzling? Would the French, or the Chinese, draw the lines in just the same places as we do? Whatever fuzziness there is in our application of words, there will be a certain fuzziness in all other languages, and the lines in all likelihood will not be drawn in just the same places. Even if the combination of these two sets of unclarities does not always make translation impossible, care and negotiation will certainly be called for in individual cases.

I think there are reasons to suppose that these difficulties are often more pressing when we try to translate and apply the terms denoting kinds of action. It is easier to know for sure the meaning of what someone else has said to you than it is to interpret what it is that they have done. For although the things people say do in part depend for their meaning on such features as context and tone of voice and literary genre, the rules and conventions here are still comparatively limited and, at least between members of the same culture, widely shared and adhered to. In their respective contexts, the meanings of what was said in one language and what is said in the proposed translation into another language can each be fairly exactly checked, even though where two cultures are very different there can be considerable difficulties in making sure that the two have the same meaning, and the fine-tuning of how to apply even these terms is always going to be to some extent unclear. But when we are dealing with action words rather than simply words for objects and abstract concepts, the situation, though similar in theory, is very much more complicated in practice. Correctly translating what is said about people's behaviour has all the general problems of translation, as well as others which are specific to actions. For it is not nearly so obvious how a person's behaviour is to be understood – what it is that they are *doing*, which action they are performing – long before one gets round to trying to see whether two pieces of behaviour in different cultures amount to morally equivalent actions.

Traditionally, the correct application of action terms requires consideration of circumstances, consequences and the agent's intention, as well as a neutral description of their behaviour – their bodily movements. Exactly when any given feature is relevant, and what kind of difference each feature makes when it is relevant, is, of course, often a matter of controversy. Even apparently trivial facts may be of significance when we come to describe what someone did – that the event took place on a Tuesday, or that they had slept badly the night before, for instance. So we need to look at the notion of 'an action'.

The moral complexity of actions

Why is the understanding of actions complex? It is not simply that action terms are fuzzy – most terms are so to a greater or lesser extent. The problem is rather that the features of what happens which might make a difference to how we should want to describe what happens are usually many more, and much more disparate than they are with words for ordinary things. 'An action' is a very elastic notion. At one extreme, the American Model Penal Code offers a minimalist definition of an action itself as 'a bodily movement whether voluntary or involuntary';[2] everything else is to be taken as a consequence of the action itself, or as a circumstance in which the action was performed, rather than considered as a feature of the action itself. This approach has the advantage of

---

[2]   *Model Penal Code*, Philadelphia, The American Law Institute, 1956, Section 1, 14.

being clear, but it is a very long way from how we would normally try to describe or classify what people do. 'All I did was move my finger' is not commonly acceptable as an account of the action performed when the finger was curled round the trigger of a powerful gun. And of course, circumstances, or consequences, are not always external irrelevancies, even if sometimes they may be. The second reason is that, since on this theory all actions-in-themselves are morally neutral, it becomes a trivial truth that the end justifies the means, whereas that is widely believed to be a highly controversial statement. Moral debate ought not to be stifled at birth in this way. Exactly when it is true that consequences and circumstances do, or do not, make a difference to what the agent actually does is a matter of considerable dispute even within our own culture.

Circumstances can make a difference to what is being said even when the same sentence is being used; similarly they can make all the difference to what is done even when the same bodily movements are taking place. So someone may spend time just sitting with a person who is very lonely; sometimes the circumstances in which this was done – for instance, that the person is her mother, or that on a particular occasion she did so despite some other pressures on her time which made doing so difficult – may well make a difference to whether we think she was being dutiful, or extremely generous, or both. Or suppose that the woman had decided to spend time with a lonely neighbour and in doing so had left her own six-year-old child alone in the house for an hour or more; that might make us see the woman's behaviour as an act of neglect rather than as an act of kindness – the circumstances of her home situation were not just a kind of incidental feature of the situation, they made all the difference to what she was doing. It is not at all clear what the most accurate description of her action might be in English. And even once what we might take to be an adequate English description has been found, there is then the usual complex of problems in translating what I would say into what the speaker of a different language, or a member of a very different culture, would say.

The role of intentions and motives is sometimes considered to be even more complex. Think of the difference between these two situations: in both, a doctor is treating a terminally ill patient, and gives her a dose of painkiller which he knows will shorten her life, but which is the minimum that will effectively relieve her pain. The treatment in both cases is within the ethical guidelines of the hospital for the appropriate care of patients at that stage in their illness. However, suppose that one of the doctors is thinking only of the patient's welfare, and judges that the comfort of her few remaining days is more important than trying to prolong matters as far as possible; and the other doctor knows that he stands to be given a considerable legacy in the terms of the patient's will, and given his urgent need of money this fact is very much in his mind. Nonetheless he gives the painkilling drug, as he would for any similarly placed patient, in a way which would not in itself incur any professional criticism. Several questions might be asked about this example, and several views taken about the right answers, and the relevance of the right answers.

Both doctors clearly foresaw that the dose of painkiller would result in the patient's death. Was that outcome unintentional? One might be inclined to say that it could not be unintentional, since that would suggest it was accidental or unforeseen, whereas both doctors would have to take responsibility for it. Or was it unintentional in the case of one doctor and not in the case of the other? For we might wish to tie 'intend' to 'desired' rather than to 'had to take responsibility for'. Are we to say that the two doctors performed the same action – administering a specific dose of morphine to a patient knowing both that it would relieve her pain and that it would shorten her life? Or does the fact that one doctor will welcome the patient's death in a way that the other does not make a difference not merely to what we might think of each of them, but to how we should think about what each of them actually *did*? Did one of them murder the patient while the other simply make her last hours more bearable and dignified? Even in our own culture, key action-related terms, such as 'intend', 'permit', 'do', and hence 'murder', are by no means clear either in their everyday or in their legal or moral uses.

There is a deep underlying pattern in all our action vocabulary; it consists of a fundamental similarity combined with what are often very significant differences which defy precise statement. Similarly, the translation of moral terms, even when it is correct, does not necessarily result in exact synonymy; what counts as the same action will not be precisely 'the same', neither physically nor even in respect of the morally relevant features.[3]

This general point can be illustrated by our use of a term such as 'marriage'. Suppose someone holds that marriages ought not to be polygamous; or that nobody should be allowed to marry at the age of thirteen; or that marriage should be between a man and a woman. Does it follow that they should then refuse to allow that the word for such relationships entered into in some other country where such unions are permitted should be translated into English as 'marriage' at all? Our practice when dealing with societies in which polygamy is permitted has certainly been to describe such unions as marriages and the partners as husband and wives. Again, an English court has recognised the relationship between a Nigerian man and a thirteen-year-old woman as a marriage. Some legislatures, for instance those of Belgium, the Netherlands and Norway recognise same-sex unions as a marriage, while in others, including England, the term 'marriage' is not used and such relationships are variously described as civil partnerships, same-sex unions, etc. [4] What lies behind this apparently verbal dispute about terminology has to do with the perceived consequences of using a particular word, which is an ever-present issue in all but the simplest cases of translation. Words come embedded in a network of associations, and using them generates expectations about what else may be implicit when they are used. In the case of 'marriage' and other such words, we might well go on to wonder what the social effects of widening the usage of so central a term will be. We might, for instance, judge that there are sufficient similarities between these various relationships to make 'marriage' the only reasonable translation, even if different groups of people have very different views of what marriage ought to be like, views which we

---

[3]   There is a more radical reason why translation might seem almost to fail altogether. For example, it would come as no surprise if it turns out that one of the very isolated Amazonian tribes has no word in their language which could translate 'insider trading'; and it would, I imagine, be quite impossible to engage in insider trading in their society. But even then, with patient negotiating, one might find parallels for concepts like 'cheating', 'not keeping a secret', 'greed', and so on, and so at least make a start at translating and explaining our term to them. Translation often involves going back to the very roots of our cultures and languages, and rebuilding from there.

[4]   In the USA, the terminology to describe such relationships varies from state to state, as do the legal consequences.

may not share. So the question arises, when is similarity important, and when does flexibility degenerate into sheer equivocation in our use of language?

Fundamentalism and 'relativism'

In discussions about morality the word 'relativism' is all too often used as a term of contempt and dismissal, somewhat in the same way as (at the opposite extreme) 'fundamentalism'. And, just as there are some people who nevertheless would proudly describe themselves as 'fundamentalists', so there are some philosophers who would willingly describe themselves as moral relativists. In both cases, such people would be insisting that there is a valuable point to be made about their position, which is not simply to be dismissed out of hand. Before we consider what fidelity to a moral tradition might require, it will be helpful to try to sort out what moral relativism and fundamentalism might be, and whether there is any middle ground between them.

Moral relativism and moral absolutism

In its strict philosophical sense, relativism asserts that actions in different cultures cannot properly be compared. A simple illustration might be seen if we think about the language used in soccer and in rugby. There are three terms which are used in both games: 'goal', 'tackle' and 'foul'. However, in soccer, to score a goal the ball must go between the posts and under the bar; in rugby, it must go over the bar. In soccer, to tackle is to try take the ball from an opposition player with only minimal contact being made, especially before making contact with the ball; in rugby, to tackle is to attempt to bring the opponent down by grabbing them, but not tripping them. A rugby-style tackle would be a blatant foul in soccer, and many fouls in soccer would be perfectly legal in rugby. Suppose, then, that someone were to ask which of the two sports has the *correct* view of what a goal, tackle and foul *really* are? The very question is absurd – there is no such thing as a goal, tackle or foul outside the conventions of each particular game. The meaning of each of these terms is relative to the rules adopted, and it does not make sense to ask which rules are the correct ones. There is no 'out there' truth to be discovered, no 'absolute' standard by which either set of rules can be shown to be closer to the truth than the other. The terms 'goal', 'tackle' and 'foul' simply have different senses within each code of football, and we can simply decide which game we wish to play. Everyone, then, will be a relativist about these rules.

The rugby/soccer example is domestic and harmless. Other examples which might be, and on occasion have been, claimed to be similar are in important ways very different. The Chinese government once said that nobody who was not Chinese could legitimately assess or criticise the practice of human rights in China. At least on the face of it, this is an instance of a pure form of moral relativism. The rules for playing Chinese-Morals are simply different from the rules for playing European- or African- or any other Morals. The different moral terms – 'rights', for instance – simply have different, non-comparable, senses in different cultures It is the *non-comparability* which is crucial. The claim is that there is no sense in asking which set of moral rules gets closer to the 'out there' moral truth, the absolute moral standard. There is no such culture-neutral moral truth, which might provide a standard for cross-cultural comparison and possible criticism. People can simply decide which moral game to play.

The fundamentalist can be thought of as taking a position about ethics which is at the other end of the spectrum. So far from it being the case that terms such as 'human rights' or 'marriage', 'lie' or 'kill' might have unrelated meanings in different moral codes, no one of them more correct than any of the others, these terms, according to the fundamentalist, are correctly understood only with reference to the correct, relevant moral facts. Of course, people can be, and often enough are, *mistaken* about what those facts are – what marriage really is, which actions really are instances of killing a human being, which are the human rights we all possess; but we must not confuse the difficulty in reaching the truth with the view that there is no absolute truth to be reached, or that moral codes, like the codes in football, are no more than human conventions which themselves depend simply on our choice. So far, then, the fundamentalist is anti-relativist. Well and good.

But the fundamentalist wishes moral truth nonetheless to be fixed in a different way as well. To support this position in a religious context fundamentalists will claim that God has revealed moral truths which will keep us from error. They typically hold that the terms which appear in moral principles can be clearly defined, and that the true principles have few if any exceptions.

Unfortunately, they often refer to principles to which there are few or no exceptions as 'absolute' principles, and hence describe anyone who believes that there might often be exceptions to moral principles as 'relativist'. But while it may be rhetorically effective to describe one's opponents as relativists, to do so betrays an important confusion. It is one thing to take the relativist view that moral principles are matters of convention, and that there is no independent 'out there' moral reality which those principles describe: it is quite another to hold that while there is indeed a moral reality which grounds true moral principles, that that moral reality is itself complex, not simple. For it is surely not morally contentious to say that often one might be obliged to behave differently in different circumstances. 'Circumstances', as the saying goes, 'alter cases.' Nor is it contentious that moral principles can often conflict; we have to decide whether to be honest or kind, or whether the children's education is more important than the health of another family member, and so on. Of course, it is perfectly possible for people to disagree about which circumstances do make a difference in this kind of way; and exactly what any such difference should be. In such cases, the disputants might be disagreeing about what ought to be done precisely because the moral quality of an action is relative to the circumstances in which it is performed; yet they would entirely accept that there is a moral truth, independent of what they might happen to think, which they are trying to discern. That is precisely not relativism.

Here is an example of a kind which is becoming more and more common. A group of violent men – say, belonging to a gang of revolutionary militia – come to the house demanding to know where John is. Suppose I know: and suppose, too, that I am quite clear that if they catch him, they will seriously injure, perhaps even kill him. Suppose I say that he left town yesterday, though I know this is not the case. There could be three rather different reactions to what I did:

1   To lie is to say something calculated to deceive. Lying is always wrong. Agonising as it might have been, I should have told the truth even in this case.

2   To lie is to say something calculated to deceive; so I lied: but the principle that one should not tell lies is one to which there are may be exceptions; it can be overridden for various reasons, in this case to save an innocent person from injury or death. It is sometimes right, and may even be one's duty, to lie.

3   What I said does not count as a lie, since those people had no right to the truth; 'to lie' means 'to say something calculated to deceive someone who on this topic has no right to the truth'. It is never right to tell a lie.

The first two define 'lie' in exactly the same way; but take a different view about whether there can be any exceptions to the principle that one ought not to tell lies. If there are no exceptions, then what I did was wrong: if there can be exceptions, then perhaps on this occasion what I did was right. The third version also agrees that what I did may have been right, but it achieves this result by making the definition of 'lie' flexible in such a way as to take different circumstances into account. Crucially, though, what (2) and (3) have in common is that they are not going to be able to spell out in advance all the possible circumstances in which, as (2) might put it, the duty not to lie is overridden, or, as (3) would say, this untruth may not count as a lie. Think of any law library; it contains volume after volume of legal cases where a court had to decide whether what someone did should count as theft, or negligence, or killing, or lack of due diligence, or whatever, because it is not obvious whether what was done fits what the law has already decided. That process of constantly refining the legal definitions is of its very nature open-ended.

The person who holds (1) would regard (3) as just mistaken, and consider even (2) as tending to moral laxism, like some version of 'situation ethics', which (it is assumed) cannot be accepted; the supporters of (2) seem to play fast and loose with the definitions of moral terms as and when they see fit. So moral rigorists will often, mistakenly, describe those who hold either (2) or (3) as 'relativist'. By contrast, the supporters of (2) or (3) would reject (1) on the grounds that it is hopelessly oversimplified. But none of these positions is relativist; they all believe there is 'out there' a correct answer, independent of whatever any particular person happens to think.

With this in mind, we can think again about the term 'marriage', which is a rather more complex example. Suppose I used to define 'marriage' as 'a legally recognised union between an adult man and an adult woman'. Now, faced with people coming into Britain from a polygamous culture, or one in which marriage can be legally recognised at, say, thirteen, there are several possible views I might take:

1   Neither of these is a marriage, nor should either be legally recognised as such in English law.
2   Neither of these two is a marriage: and for that reason no British resident may attempt to contract such a marriage: if they do they can be prosecuted for bigamy, where appropriate, or for having sexual relations with a minor.
3   Nevertheless, while (2) remains true, there may be good reasons why English law should recognise such contracts in the case of people who entered into them legally in their own countries. And it may be simplest to *describe* them as 'marriages'.
4   Both of these in some circumstances might truly be marriages; the stricter requirements which we make in our culture need not be significant in every culture, or indeed in any other culture. Their circumstances may in some important way be different.

A similar range of positions could be considered in the case of same-sex partnerships. The issue is not just a verbal one about the definition of moral terms, such as 'marriage' and the rest. It is rather about our perceptions of the moral world; for it is these which in the end govern the interpretation of our moral principles and of the terms in which they are couched. No moral principle guarantees its correct application, no matter how detailed it may be, since moral concepts are in themselves fuzzy, and moral principles can conflict with one another, in which case some reconciliation has to be found. None of these four positions need be relativist; but in various ways they try to take the complexity of some moral situations into account. And so in other issues as well. May one lie to save someone's life, kill in self-defence, be cruel to be kind? Are unemployment benefits more important than pensions if the economy cannot afford both?

Moral pluralism

There are good grounds for saying that all moral codes must be at some level comparable. That is to say, there are correct standards for human conduct by which the moral beliefs of any individual, or culture, or society can in principle be judged. Ethics is surely about how people should live, and live together; and the point of living a morally good life is that it will normally be a life of personal fulfilment and interpersonal respect and harmony.[5] The objective limitation on any acceptable moral code is that it will involve an attempt to meet human needs. At least at a basic level, these needs are common to us all. But this does not necessarily imply that everyone should live in exactly the same way. We humans differ from other animals in the sheer complexity of the needs we have learned, and of the very different ways in which those needs can genuinely be met. I suppose that I could have led a fulfilled life had I made quite different choices of career and lifestyle, or had I lived in a very different culture. Different societies will develop different moral codes according to their circumstances – of climate, the level of industrialisation, the attitudes of neighbouring societies, and so on. I see no reason to suppose that all the truly fulfilling ways of organising one's life, or structuring a society, will have to be identical. Indeed, as our legal systems suggest, they are almost never identical, and can at times differ quite markedly. There is a good case for pluralism in ethics, given the complexity and adaptability of humans. But the key anti-relativist move is to say that the fact that we humans share a common nature places some limits on what kinds of personal and social structures will be genuinely fulfilling. It is this common basis which entitles people in one culture to assess, and sometimes criticise, the code of a different culture – for instance because it systematically undervalues

---

[5]   'Normally'; for even morally blameless people can be afflicted with such a degree of physical or mental ill-health that to speak of their life as 'fulfilled' would be quite mistaken.

women, or has no place for the arts, or is heedless of the needs of future generations. The whole notion of human rights depends on the fact that all human beings have basic needs in common, even though these can up to a point be satisfied in different ways.

Ethics, then, is non-relativist and pluralist. From the first it follows that translation from one moral code to another ought to be possible, because at a deep level we humans all have the same basic needs, which provide the basis of mutual comprehension. From the second it follows that translation from one culture to another need not be easy, and sometimes will be very difficult. The difference in our circumstances, personalities and abilities means that we will have to live rather different lives if we are to be fulfilled. 'What would be the equivalent of that behaviour in my culture, and in my circumstances?' is neither a senseless question, nor one to which the answer is always going to be obvious. The diagram I used in Chapter 2 to schematise the relationships between sentences in different languages is equally appropriate here in thinking about the relationships between actions in different cultures.

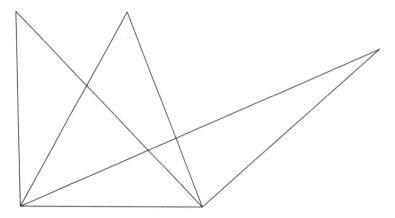

The relationship between three hypothetical cultures, each represented by a triangle

1   There is an area which all three triangles share, which we can take as representing those features of human nature which are common to us all. This common human nature is the basis on which all values can be assessed; this renders ethics absolutist rather than relativist.

2   But ethics as represented in this diagram is pluralist: that is
to say, there is more than one way, building on the common
base, in which human nature can truly be fulfilled.
3   Some cultures are a good deal closer to one another than to
others – in this case, the two triangles to left overlap more
than either does with the third.
4   At the tips the differences are great, in two cases very great,
yet still not incomparably so.

The diagram is, of course, oversimplified, in that it does not exhibit
the fact that some, and perhaps all, cultures will contain some
patterns of behaviour which are *not* morally admirable, and hence
not effective ways of fulfilling our shared human nature.

Pluralism and relativism: a summary

Relativism

- Different moral codes define their values internally.
- They cannot be compared with one another on any
  neutral basis. Any given moral code can be criticised
  only from within.

Absolutism

- The truth of moral principles is independent of
  whether or not people believe they are true. Moral
  truth is 'objective'.
- NB This has nothing to do with how simple moral
  principles are, whether they have exceptions, etc.
- It is simply an assertion of basic comparability. The
  question is whether this claim can be backed up.

Pluralism

- Relativism is false. Hence, pluralism is one form of
  absolutism.
- There can be more than one defensible moral code,
  and perhaps more than one true moral code – more
  than one *successful* way for a society to structure the
  conditions for living a fulfilled life.

- Such codes will be genuinely different, incompatible in practice, yet basically comparable.

What moral relativism is not
None of the following views is relativist: absolutists can and usually do hold them.

(*1*) *In different circumstances, people will often have to behave differently.* Of course one may discuss which circumstances should make a difference.

(2) *Few if any moral principles apply in the same way in all situations.* In most situations, several relevant considerations are involved.

(3) *People ought to act according to their sincerely held moral beliefs.* Of course they should; but this does not say that their beliefs are always correct. Almost nobody's moral beliefs are always correct!

Grounds for moral pluralism

(1) Pluralism of the equally defensible
 – Factual ignorance: in medicine, genetic research, economic policy.
 – Philosophical uncertainty: status of a fetus; moment of death.
(2) Pluralism of the equally true
 – Different views on what is morally significant.
 – Different priorities within what is agreed as relevant.
 – Different viable cultures.
 – Different social structures; hence different views on some rights.

What do we mean by the imitation of Christ?

The imitation of Christ is a venerable Christian ideal going back to very early times indeed. In Acts, Luke presents the ministry of the first Christians almost as a recapitulation of the ministry, trial,

death and resurrection of Jesus himself. The apostles heal the sick
and preach the good news just as Jesus did. The description of the
martyrdom of Stephen is full of details selected to heighten the
similarity to the trial and death of Jesus. The way in which Peter
escapes from prison and is welcomed by a woman from the
Christian community is told in such a way as to remind the reader
of the escape of Jesus from the tomb and his appearing first to the
women.[6] Paul, in emphasising that Christians are the body of
Christ, and exhorting his communities to imitate him as he imitates
Christ,[7] surely contributed to the ideal of the imitation of Christ as
it was developed.

Not surprisingly, however, the ways in which this ideal was
applied varied very considerably. In the context in which Paul uses
the phrase he is concerned with the various ways in which the
Corinthians treat one another, and appeals to the fact that they
should remember that they share in the one Eucharist, bread and
cup (1 Cor. 10:16; 11:23–29). They cannot be discerning the body
of Christ if they share in pagan sacrifices, or ignore the needs of
their own poorer brothers and sisters, when they purport to be
sharing in the supper of the Lord while refusing to share their food
with those who are more needy than they are. In later centuries,
Christ was seen as a model in notably different ways: a more
ascetical tendency in the Eastern Churches stressed the way in
which Jesus the man renounced all merely human comforts, suffering in obedience to his Father, and so showing us the path which we
too must follow to attain union with God. In the late medieval West,
Thomas à Kempis's famous manual of devotion, *The Imitation of
Christ*, expressed the ideals of the Brotherhood of the Common
Life, who sought to imitate the communal simplicity of early
Christian community as described in Acts 4:32–37. The imitation
of Christ involved an attention to the needs of the time: preaching a
life of apostolic simplicity, combined with a love of Christian
learning. Ignatius Loyola in his *Spiritual Exercises* encourages the
person making the exercises to pray 'to choose to be poor with
Christ poor, to suffer opprobrium with Christ who endured so

---

[6]   Acts 2:37—4:22 (preaching and healing); 6:8—7:60 (trial and imprisonment);
      12:1–18 (escape from prison).
[7]   1 Cor. 11:1.

much of it, rather than honours ...'; Ignatius thought he needed to emphasise these attitudes as a counter to the unbridled ambition, secular and ecclesiastical, of too many of his contemporaries.[8]

One might first reflect that it is not at all clear that Jesus was poor, nor that his family was, nor that his whole life was a life of suffering and deprivation. I say this for two reasons. The first is to point out what is evident here and rather more generally, that the factual basis for various aspects of the life of Jesus deserving of imitation needs to be rather carefully controlled by what we do know of Jesus from the New Testament; and secondly that there is inevitably going to be a process of selection to determine which features of the life of Jesus are to be imitated, and what it is about these features that makes them important rather than others. The process of selecting and precisely identifying is not a simple one, nor is it a purely mechanical one. In these key respects it is a kind of translation procedure, which has to start with an understanding of the original, and cannot be oversimplified without distortion.

To illustrate the point, we might consider the Last Supper. What exactly was Jesus doing? The Gospels are not agreed on whether the supper was eaten on the evening of Passover or not, since the trials of Jesus, recounted as taking place the next day, could not have taken place on the Passover day. So it is not entirely clear whether Jesus celebrated a Passover meal or not, though that is certainly how many early Christians liked to think of it. In any event, it appears that Jesus did something unusual both before and after the meal; he did so not just once, but on two *separate* occasions 'while they were at table' and 'when supper was ended'. He took first bread and, later, a cup of wine, and related each of them to his imminent death: his body would be 'given'; his blood would be 'poured out'. It seems to me that above all he was trying to give his disciples a way of understanding what would otherwise for them have been a totally devastating event, the death of someone they had learned to think of as the promised Messiah. He tried to reassure them by using the meal to interpret his death in traditional terms – the sacrifice of Isaac, obedient unto the point of

---

[8]   Ignatius Loyola, *Spiritual Exercises* (167; 116). For illuminating reflections on how these and other similar phrases are to be read, see Philip Endean, 'On poverty with Christ poor', *The Way* 47/1–2 (January–April 2008), pp. 47–66.

death, and yet saved by God;[9] and the blood of a new covenant with God, who even in the darkest times does not forget his chosen ones. He hoped his disciples would be able to see his death as something other than pointless and catastrophic. Perhaps also he himself felt the need to be understood and supported in the ordeal he faced. He tried twice to get this lesson across, as if for the disciples it had not really sunk in the first time. His death, he said, could be seen as a new Passover, the start of a new exodus, the entry into the Kingdom. It may also be that in asking the disciples to do this 'in memory of me' he was not asking *them* to remember him in future; the Aramaic phrase he used – 'as a reminder' – expressed a prayer that *God* might remember the person making the prayer; so the Church would in our own day pray that God might 'look upon this sacrifice, and see the victim whose death has reconciled us to yourself'. That would explain Paul's way of putting it, that the disciples were 'proclaiming the death of the Lord until he comes'. [10] They repeated Jesus' prayer because it was still centrally important for them to make that same prayer, which defined at once their belief and their hopes; they were not performing a kind of memorial service because he had asked them to. Like the Corinthians, the Church now prays that, as we beg God to remember the death of his Son, so we, 'nourished by his body and blood, may become one body and one spirit in Him'.

For us to be faithful to what Jesus did, then, involves first of all trying as best we can to understand exactly what it was that Jesus did; and then trying to discern which aspects of his behaviour are the important ones for us if we are to do something that would be our equivalent, expressed in a way which communicates with us in our time and in our various cultures. The aim is that we all find our places in the history of salvation as it develops over time: genuine translation, then, not mimicry. We will have to do both less and more than what took place on that night.

Much the same goes for other things that Jesus certainly did: being familiar with sinners and outcasts; criticising some of the religious authorities for misunderstanding their own traditions;

---

9   See above, p. 88.
10 See Fritz Chenderlin ,'Do this as my memorial: the semantic and conceptual background and value of *anamnesis* in 1 Corinthians 11:24–25', *Analecta Biblica*, 1983.

listening to foreigners and outsiders such as Samaritans, the Roman centurion and the Canaanite woman in Tyre; finding effective ways of communicating with the people to whom he was sent; praying; being willing to die rather than swerve from his vocation. Contemporary Christians are sometimes surprised, even shocked, to discover how totally Jewish Jesus was, and therefore the extent to which, were we to be transported back to first-century Palestine, we would have found him extremely strange. One of the problems with fundamentalists is that they so often fail to come to terms with the ways in which Jesus was *not* like us, did *not* speak like us, did *not* live in our world, did *not* face our complex problems; in short, would never have done things which to us would seem entirely ordinary.

We have to accept, then, that the imitation of Christ which is an ideal for any Christian provides us with only very general guidance in our day-to-day affairs. This is hardly surprising, since it is clear that he was much more interested in emphasising the need for repentance in view of the coming Kingdom than he was in spelling out anything resembling an ethical theory, or a detailed recipe for daily living. Much of his ethical teaching consisted in rejecting the obsessive legalism of some of his contemporaries, in emphasising the importance of mutual forgiveness, and in urging upon us a concern for the poor and the outcast. His mission, and his awareness of its likely end, acted as a focus for his teaching, leading him to concentrate on things that were really urgent as well as essential. Thus the beatitudes are assurances for the downtrodden and the poor, for those who, as peacemakers or seekers after justice, were being unjustly treated: God will vindicate them; theirs is the Kingdom of heaven. The message is like that of the parable of the rich man and the beggar at his door, not so much a blueprint for our contemporary Christian life, but a promise that the disciples who suffer in his name will in the end be vindicated by God. Of course, we can indeed draw a moral lesson for ourselves; we should never maltreat those who seek for justice, or oppress the poor and the weak; we should sympathise with those who mourn. Things which Jesus said in one context can be transferred by us to other contexts as well. But the transfer needs to be carefully done. We may indeed seek to be 'poor in spirit' or peacemakers; but we should not, as it seems to me, actively seek to be persecuted for the sake of justice, or to be mourners ourselves. The beatitudes are promises, not moral principles.

7

Fidelity to a Moral Tradition: Living as They Lived?

Some (comparatively) uncontroversial examples

The constraints on fidelity to a moral tradition and on the faithful translation of texts across centuries and cultures are fundamentally the same. The first essential is to have a grasp of what was done at the various stages of that tradition. To achieve this, one has to have an accurate understanding of the conventions governing the interpretation of that piece of behaviour at the time. When we try to think about what people did centuries ago in very different cultures and circumstances, we clearly cannot negotiate with them as we can and do negotiate with our own contemporaries in order to find out what they are doing; so our understanding of their behaviour is inevitably often going to be less than complete. Despite the difficulties, however, translation is an everyday activity, and one which we often carry out with fair success. So we may reasonably hope that, when it is undertaken with due seriousness, imagination and care, we will reach reliable results most of the time. We already have a good grasp of potential pitfalls, and to be forewarned is to be forearmed. And though such translation may well be more complicated when we are trying to understand past actions in our terms, for the reasons I have given, the process is not, I suggest, in principle different. There is no reason to suppose that we have no way of identifying what it is to be faithful to a tradition of how we should live.

We can also often readily spot dreadful attempts by people who are desperate to do what they hope is the right thing in a culture with which they are not really familiar. Once in Zimbabwe I stood up out of politeness when a young woman, daughter of the household, came into the room where I was sitting with a friend of mine talking with her mother. What I took for politeness prompted an instant torrent of explanation in Shona from my friend, because, all unwittingly, I had given the impression that on no account would I allow the young woman to stand there in a position superior to me. My polite gesture was read as arrogance, expressing a total lack of respect for their hospitality. Again, we have all seen elderly people trying and conspicuously failing to behave like people half their age, for instance, fallaciously assuming that some kind of literal imitation is the recipe for success. In general, we need to learn to distinguish between absurd mimicry and genuine translation from one culture to another. So much, then, for some simple stage setting. Here are some more serious examples.

Closeness to sinners and the outcast

What was it in Jesus' way of living that his critics found so objectionable? One thing was that he ate with tax collectors and sinners.[1] More precisely, we must ask what was it they found objectionable about eating with tax collectors. At this point we have to speculate, since the texts do not specifically tell us. Tax collectors collected taxes on behalf of the Roman administration; and perhaps, since the Romans were regarded as hostile to the Jewish religion, their collaborators were pre-eminent examples of sinners: tax collectors made common cause with alien occupiers and collaborated with people who were hostile to the true religion. Perhaps also, since they had to make their own living out of collecting taxes, it was commonly thought that tax collectors were extortionate in their demands.

There are perhaps three questions we might ask.

The first question is whether we are to suppose that Jesus agreed that tax collectors were sinners, or whether his willingness to associate with them was a criticism of the Pharisees' over-rigid view of what was sinful? Perhaps. But in all three Gospels the phrase 'tax collectors and sinners' sounds very much as if the connection is simply taken for granted: tax collectors are just like that, sinners. It is also difficult to say definitely whether Jesus would have criticised them for collaboration or for extortion or for both. But at any rate in the mind of the evangelists, the tax collectors were sinners, and they give us no reason to suppose that

---

[1] Mark 2:13–17; Matt. 9:9–13; Luke 5:27–32.

Jesus thought of them differently. Jesus eats with people he believes to be sinners on the grounds that obviously it is sinners who have to be called to repentance, just as it is the sick, not the healthy, who need a doctor.[2] In that case, we might perhaps learn to follow his lead by not adopting the comfortable policy of preaching only to people who agree with us already.

Or did the Pharisees object to *any* contact with such sinners, even in an attempt to preach repentance to them? Was Jesus perhaps altogether too familiar and comfortable with them? If that is the point, we might take Jesus to be teaching by example that denunciation from a distance, whether justified or not, certainly is not the best way to win people's hearts; a lesson which many contemporary Christians and Churches could well relearn. We can then ask what we should make of people who collaborate with our enemies, or our religious opponents, or who practise extortion on others. Do we refuse to deal with people whose views differ in important ways from our own? Devout believers in many religions tend to find it genuinely difficult to engage with the members of a pluralist society whose convictions on some sensitive issues they simply do not share. Do we approve of a policy of not talking to enemies, political opponents, or their perhaps disreputable friends – talking even to terrorists? Should we ever excommunicate sinners? The gospel narrative does not in itself tell us what for each of us will be a good 'translation' of Jesus' attitude to sinners; translation requires that we understand not merely the original, but also the nuances of the language into which it is to be translated. Just so with learning to find our own equivalents for what Jesus did.

Another episode involving Jesus, his Pharisee host, and a woman in some ways raises similar issues. The first thing to notice is that whereas Luke explains that the woman is a sinner, and that her washing Jesus' feet with her tears, drying them with her hair, and anointing them, are all acts of loving repentance, Mark and Matthew say nothing about her being a sinner, nor do they see the anointing as an act of repentance, but as an act of reverence; John tells a very similar story, except that this time the woman is Mary, sister of Martha and Lazarus, and she is anticipating the anointing

---

[2] Luke 5:30–32.

of Jesus for his burial.[3] It is hard to know whether underlying all these accounts we have just a single event or not. If it is, then here we have an excellent example of how a single piece of behaviour can be interpreted as being one or more quite different actions. Or perhaps we have here one example of the early Christians – the four evangelists in this case – each putting a very different slant upon an episode in order to make a point which they thought would be especially illuminating for their particular readership. In all four episodes, the woman is accused of wasting money on an expensive gesture instead of giving money to the poor. Three Gospels see the episode as a kind of prefiguring of Jesus' passion (after his death he was not immediately anointed); reverence, therefore, cannot be valued in purely financial terms: Luke sees it as an act of total and loving repentance, and, in order to do so, presents the woman as a sinner, and Jesus' host as thinking that if Jesus is at all who he claims to be, he surely ought to have known what kind of woman she was. Jesus contrasts her love and the experience of forgiveness which accompanies it with the rather formal reception given to him by Simon, his host. Sinners are to be welcomed, their advances encouraged, their extravagant gestures gratefully understood and received.

I have used these examples in order to emphasise that even in comparatively uncontroversial instances of the moral tradition which goes back to Jesus, we still have to make something of an effort to understand what the original people were actually *doing*; and we need to do that *before* we then try to see what fidelity to his example might require of us. This example is simple enough: the implications for method are nonetheless crucially important. Even such a simple exercise as reflecting on these straightforward examples can raise some perhaps uncomfortable questions about our own conduct as his disciples.

Collaboration and revolution

It is not clear whether or not it was because the tax collectors could be seen as collaborating with the occupying regime that made Jesus' act of sitting at table with them so objectionable to the

---

[3]   Mark 14:3–9; Matt. 26:6–13; Luke 7:36–50.

Pharisees. But there is no doubt that collaborationism was the issue explicitly raised by the Pharisees and Herodians who came to entrap Jesus with the question, 'Is it lawful to pay taxes to Caesar or not?'[4] What did Jesus mean when, having been shown the coin with the Emperor's head on it, he replied, 'Well then, give to Caesar what belongs to him, and to God what belongs to God'? Some subsequent generations of Christians have tried to use this text as the basis of a whole theory of Church–State relations. Christians in the United States have used it to justify the strict separation of Church and State in their Constitution; other Christians have claimed that the reply was a refusal to accept that there need be any conflict or confrontation at all, and that harmonious co-existence was what was needed; or have claimed that what Jesus was condemning was a kind of religious revolution against the secular power. Once more, there can be no solution to the problem 'How are we to remain faithful to the teachings of Jesus?' until we have sorted out what sayings like this one actually meant. But this time, perhaps, a good deal depends on the tone of voice in which it was said, which, in the case of a saying reproduced in an ancient document, is not so easy to reconstruct.

I think at least a case can be made for saying that this remark of Jesus contains very little teaching indeed. The situation is explicitly described as one in which Jesus' enemies set out to entrap him into plumping for one side or the other of a highly contentious issue. The questioners were not interested in the truth; and, as commentators have often remarked with some frustration, it is not as though Jesus' answer is at all clear; he does not even attempt to define what might belong to Caesar and what to God. So maybe we should see this as one place where understanding what was said crucially depends on context and tone of voice. Jesus was being asked a trick question by people who were not interested in the truth: trick questions don't deserve a serious answer. Jesus gave them a completely diplomatic reply, pointing out the choices they themselves had made, while deftly avoiding the trap and committing himself to nothing in particular. If we have anything to learn, it is not about a keystone of political theory, but rather when not to try to answer questions head on. Translated into contemporary terms,

---

[4]   Mark 12:13–17; Matt. 22:15–22; Luke 20:20–26.

it might be a model of how to behave at a hostile press conference, but not at all a serious recipe for the guidance of a Christian political tradition.

Relations between churches

In the Acts of the Apostles, Luke gives us accounts of two episodes in the experience of the early Christian churches, one of which is also handed down to us as it was seen through the eyes of Paul, in his letter to the Galatians.[5] The issue, as all three accounts of these episodes agree, was whether Gentile converts to Christianity should be bound to observe the requirements of the Jewish Law, especially those concerning diet and circumcision. The difficulties in understanding what was done, and hence the meaning of what was agreed, are rather more pressing than they were in either of the examples we have just looked at. But the method and aims are the same: to work from that understanding towards an account of what it might be for us to be faithful to that tradition in our very different circumstances.

The earliest of the relevant texts is Paul's account in his letter to the Galatians. He is intent upon making several different points: first, that Christians who are not ethnic Jews should not be bound by any of the specific requirements of the traditional Jewish Law: in particular, that they should not have to be circumcised and that they should not have to observe the dietary requirements. Second, Paul is insisting that his authority is just as God-given as is that of Peter or the other leaders of the church in Jerusalem; and third, he is committed to unity and collaboration between the churches; he shakes hands with the leaders of the Jerusalem church, James, Peter, and John, and he promises that the church in Antioch will try to assist the financially struggling church in Jerusalem.

Luke wrote his Gospel–Acts perhaps thirty years after Paul wrote that letter to the Galatians, and gives his own 'take' on the same controversies. In the first place, he gives an elaborate account of how it came about that Peter came to see that the Gospel was intended not simply for the Jews but for the Gentiles as well – people whom Peter had previously regarded as ritually unclean.

[5]   Acts 10; 15:1–35; Gal. 2:1–14.

Just as Ananias had a vision telling him to go and fetch the newly converted Saul/Paul to Damascus, so the Roman centurion Cornelius had a vision telling him to go and fetch Peter: like Paul, Peter himself was 'converted' by a vision in which he saw all the creatures of creation, and heard God insisting that none of them was to be thought of as 'unclean'. When Peter met Cornelius and preached the Gospel to him along with his entire household, they were all overcome by the Spirit in such a manner that Peter and his Jewish companions could not but recognise that astonishing fact and baptise them immediately. Perhaps this is Luke's way of saying that Peter and Paul were indeed equals, and that their shared policy towards Gentiles was born of an experience which was in essentials the same for each of them. Interestingly, Peter's vision legitimating the inclusion of the Gentiles is given in terms of the animals God created, and so could well also symbolise the abandonment of the Jewish food laws, which was the other point of later controversy between Peter and Paul.

Luke also mentions the controversy between some of the Jewish members of the Jerusalem church and the Christians in Paul's church in Antioch: but he does not put it in terms of a violent disagreement between Peter and Paul, nor, contrary to what Paul claims in Galatians, is there any hint that Peter yielded to undue pressure from the Jewish party in Jerusalem on the issue of the food laws. Indeed, Luke presents Peter as Paul's strongest supporter. But Luke also says, as Paul nowhere does, that the Jerusalem church insisted on a kind of compromise on the issue of the food laws. What is clear enough is that the Jewish Christians were being asked to reject their own God-given traditions to be at one with people who would not accept what they regarded as key elements of the unrevoked law of God – just the kind of point which some Christians of a later age might leap to regard as a question of heresy with which they should have nothing whatever to do.

So how should we translate these aspects of our tradition into contemporary terms? As usual, the key is to try to isolate which elements seem to be essential in the tradition. Here I would suggest that there are four:

1   The overriding conviction that the Gospel is intended for everyone.

2   The criterion for full acceptance by the Christian community is neither the faith-history of the person, nor is it the details of their current religious observances.
3   The decisive criterion is that one can discern the fruits of the Spirit, and can do so even in people one might think of as outsiders, or in some important ways contravening what we ourselves have regarded as the clearly revealed will of God.
4   There is a concern for mutual acceptance and mutual assistance even between churches with very different histories, authorities and customs.

The first of these might seem obvious to us. But it dawned only gradually: even Jesus in his own ministry told his disciples to preach only to the towns of Israel; he was only reluctantly persuaded otherwise by the Syro-Phoenician woman, and by the Roman centurion. In both cases he was moved by their manifest faith. Just before Mark gives his account of the meeting with the woman, he reports a dispute between Jesus and the Pharisees, in which Jesus seems to abolish the whole teaching about unclean foods. And the parable of the good Samaritan precisely uses the shock value of praising an outsider – which was how the Jews regarded Samaritans – to emphasise the universality of God's love which we should try to emulate.[6]

Yet the disputes between the early Christian churches in Antioch and Jerusalem were not resolved by enforcing one uniform practice for all. Those who had been led to Christianity through their Jewish heritage and their recognition of Jesus as the Jewish Messiah were permitted to retain the Jewish practices of their tradition; but those practices were not forced on people who had come to Christianity by some route other than Judaism. The ways in which the Gentile Christians thought of Jesus were much less Jewish in language and style than those in use by the first Jewish Christians. No one saw the importance of accepting such differences more clearly than Paul the Pharisee, himself once an 'outsider' par excellence in Christian eyes who was at first accepted only reluctantly. What they all looked for was the gifts of the Spirit: where

---

[6]   Mark 7:24–30 for the Syro-Phoenician woman; Matt. 15:24 for the restriction of Jesus' ministry; Mark 7:19 for the background; Luke 10:25–37 for the parable of the good Samaritan.

those gifts were to be found, admission to the Christian community was not to be in dispute.[7] So communities very different in style and practice were at pains to remain in fellowship in such a way that differences of past history and religious traditions were acknowledged and accepted, and to express their unity in practical ways, such as the collection which Paul encouraged his church in Antioch to continue to contribute to the poor church in Jerusalem.

The fundamentalist might be tempted to say that what we have to learn from these early elements in our tradition can be simply translated into our terms: we should indeed be willing to preach to the Gentiles as well as to the Jews; we should not insist upon circumcision and Jewish dietary laws, though these customs can perhaps be retained by Jewish converts; and there's an end to it. To try to learn any wider lessons can only lead to religious indifferentism. Thinking along such lines, the Roman Catholic Church took almost three centuries before it fully accepted the need of applying precisely these lessons to the new converts in China; after an initial period in which it was all in favour of adaptability and integration, it later retreated to a fundamentalist attitude which did serious damage to the preaching of the Gospel in the process, and from which the Chinese church is perhaps only today beginning to be allowed to recover. Contrary to the practice of Peter and Paul, different religious histories, issuing in different cultural symbols, were simply excluded. The respect shown to Confucius, the Chinese sage, and the Chinese rites of veneration and respect towards their ancestors were no more incompatible with Christian faith than were circumcision and the dietary laws of Judaism. The problems of translation of Christian beliefs and texts into a very different non-Western language, and of trying to discover how Christianity was to be lived by people notably different from ourselves, were seen as fatal obstacles standing in the way of fidelity to Catholic tradition. Efforts by Jesuit missionaries and Chinese scholars to negotiate and adjust possible translations, sympathetically regarded at first, were in the end simply dismissed or ignored. It was as though only word-for-word transliteration and the mimicry of the rites of a Western version of the Church could satisfy the Western authorities. Differences such as those between

---

[7] Acts 10:43.

the preaching and language of Jesus and that of Paul, or that of Paul and that of the Fourth Gospel, differences which the early churches were clear-sighted enough to welcome, were ruled out as clearly unacceptable when it came to the task of translating Christianity into language and customs intelligible to seventeenth- and eighteenth-century China.[8] In a very similar way, the ecumenical movement between the Christian churches, though theoretically endorsed almost on all sides, has been actively discouraged from attempts to transcend fundamentalist attitudes to tradition, translation and rites; and the resulting divisions in fact impede the preaching of the Gospel. We simply lack the courage and vision of Peter and Paul, Jerusalem and Antioch.

Some less simple examples

Pacifism

If one asks how we should today be faithful to Christian tradition when it comes to questions of war and peace, it is at once clear that there has been no agreement across the centuries. The sayings of Jesus on the topic are among the best known in the Gospels:

> 'You have heard that it was said, "An eye for an eye and a tooth for a tooth." But I say to you, Do not resist the evildoer. But if anyone strikes you on the right cheek, turn the other also ...
>
> 'You have heard that it was said, "You shall love your neighbour and hate your enemy." But I say to you, Love your enemies and pray for those who persecute you, so that you may be children of your Father in heaven, for he makes his sun to rise on the evil and on the good, and sends rain on the righteous and on the unrighteous.'
>
> Suddenly, one of those with Jesus put his hand to his sword, drew it, and struck the slave of the high priest, cutting off his ear. Then Jesus said to him, 'Put your sword back into its place. For all who take the sword shall perish by the sword.'[9]

---

8   An illuminating but also chastening collection of the relevant decrees is to be found in Ray R. Noll (ed.), *100 Roman Documents concerning the Chinese Rites Controversy (1645–1941)* (Ricci Institute for Chinese-Western Cultural History, University of San Francisco, 1992).

9   Matt. 5:38–39, 43–45; 26:51–52.

There is an echo of this in Paul:

> *Do not repay anyone evil for evil, but take thought for what is noble in the sight of all. If it is possible, so far as it depends on you, live peaceably with all; beloved, never avenge yourselves, but leave room for the wrath of God; for it is written, 'Vengeance is mine, I will repay, says the Lord.' No, if your enemies are hungry, feed them; if they are thirsty, give them something to drink, 'for by doing this you will be heaping coals on their heads.' Do not be overcome by evil, but overcome evil with good.*[10]

It is important to notice what are the reasons which are given for these very testing demands upon the believer. In both Matthew and Luke, the motivation is to reflect the goodness of God; Matthew spells this out in terms of the even-handedness of God's love for all his creation; Luke emphasises the mercy of God, perhaps echoing the Lord's Prayer for forgiveness as we forgive others. Despite the slightly vindictive-sounding quotation of the proverb by Paul, it seems that his motivation is somehow to win over one's enemies by kindness. Maybe the coals of fire are thought of in connection with a furnace for removing the impurities in metals. In any event, the basic motivation is in terms of witnessing, and perhaps also inspiring repentance, by giving an example of loving forgiveness. The way in which Jesus accepted his own death would be the role model for his followers. In so far as Paul is concerned, and perhaps more generally, the belief that the end-time was near made it easier to adopt a policy which might have immense impact on others but whose longer-term effects did not need to be considered. This approach is clear elsewhere in Paul, when he argues in favour of the view that if someone were not already married it might be better not to consider marriage at all.[11] So perhaps the heroic example given by Christians refusing to resist enemies might contribute to a final willingness to accept the Kingdom of God.

But as the years passed, the force of such reasons would certainly have diminished. And indeed we find that other considera-

---

[10]   Rom. 12:17–21; he cites Prov. 25:21–22.
[11]   1 Cor. 7:25–39, where this is explicitly stated; indeed perhaps the entire chapter has to be read against this background.

tions were in fact invoked, at least so far as Christians in military service were concerned. Soldiers had to take an oath to the Emperor, and were often required to take part in ceremonies which implied that the Emperor was worshipped as a god. Tertullian argued against them doing so, for obvious reasons, pointing out that Jesus taught that no one can serve two masters. Origen argued that the Emperor would be more effectively helped by the prayers of Christians than by their military services. But Athanasius argues that even killing can in some circumstances be right, and Ambrose spells this out in some detail:

> *It is clear, then, that [the moral virtues] are related to one another. For courage, which in war preserves one's country from the barbarians, or at home defends the weak, or comrades from robbers, is full of justice; and to know on what plan to defend and to give help, how to make use of opportunities of time and place, is the part of prudence and moderation, and temperance itself cannot observe due measure without prudence. To know a fit opportunity, and to make return according to what is right, belongs to justice. In all these, too, large-heartedness is necessary, and fortitude of mind, and often of body, so that we may carry out what we wish.*[12]

The way in which prudence, temperance and moderation are treated here are strongly reminiscent of Aristotle's *Nicomachean Ethics* rather than any other Christian source.[13] There were some hesitations about such adaptive policies, however. Gregory of Nazianzen sits rather on the fence, while somehow implying that the fighting soldier was not altogether blameless:

> *Homicide in war is not reckoned by our Fathers as homicide; I presume this from their wish to make concession to men fighting on behalf of chastity and true religion. Perhaps, however, it is well to counsel that those whose hands are not clean only abstain from communion for three years.*

---

[12] Three Books on the Duties of the Clergy, Book 1, Chapter XXVII, 129.
[13] See, for instance, NE VI, 2, 1144a6–9, and VI, 13 1144b32–1145a2. Moral virtues (Ambrose mentions three cardinal virtues courage, justice and temperance) and the intellectual virtue of practical wisdom have to work hand in hand. 'Measure' here means the appropriate response to a situation.

Augustine, too, is not entirely comfortable. He suggests:

> *If it is supposed that God could not enjoin warfare, because in after times it was said by the Lord Jesus Christ, 'I say unto you, That ye resist not evil: but if any one strike thee on the right cheek, turn to him the left also,' the answer is, that what is here required is not a bodily action, but an inward disposition.*[14]

Augustine clearly sees the need to explain how his conclusion is to be reconciled with the Gospel text. Gregory of Nazianzen sees that there is a problem, but gives no clue as to how he might resolve it. A rather more direct attempt to meet the difficulty is offered by Thomas Aquinas. Having set out what he takes to be the three conditions which have to be met before it could be right to engage in a war, he deals explicitly with the fact that such a conclusion seems to be excluded by the words of Jesus himself. Aquinas accommodates the saying of Jesus about those who take the sword and will perish by the sword by arguing that an individual who acts on the authority of his prince, or of a judge, or at the command of God, is acting on that authority; it is therefore not he himself who 'takes the sword'. Furthermore, the person who takes up the sword must do so with reluctance and only when it is essential to do so. Aquinas also suggests that to defeat an evildoer might lead him to abandon his sinful ways, which would therefore be to benefit the evildoer, not to harm him. And finally, that to fight when it is justifiable is not to act against peace, except in the sense in which Jesus himself said he did not come to bring peace but the sword. To fight a justified war is to work for true peace.

In so far as this argument offers to explain what the sayings of Jesus meant, it is surely less than successful; and the hope that a war might lead the enemy to abandon his evil ways is of little help if the enemy is killed in battle. What in fact the argument demonstrates is that Aquinas, living in a period in which war in Europe was endemic, simply believed that under the stringent conditions in which he thought war to be justified the prohibitions of Jesus simply had to be overridden. The subsequent just war tradition has

---

[14]   *Against Faustus*, 22.76. For this and the several other references here, I am indebted to Daniel H. Shubin, *Militarist Christendom and the Gospel of the Prince of Peace*, 2nd rev. edn (2007), pp. 31–47, posted on the internet at http://christianpacificism.com.

proceeded along similar lines. Some critics have argued that in the modern nuclear age, the just war theory itself is simply outdated. At least as it seems to me, this is a simple confusion: what their arguments really would show, were they accepted, is that according to the just war theory itself, many, perhaps most, modern wars are illegitimate, not that the theory itself is useless. So the only unanswered criticisms of the view that war at least in principle can be legitimate are put forward by contemporary pacifists, among whom those who are Christians would still wish to insist on the straightforward sense of all but one of the sayings of Jesus.

This example well illustrates a more general set of issues, which we touched upon earlier.[15] Consider four statements in the Sermon on the Mount:

> *'If your right eye causes you to sin, tear it out and throw it away.'*

> *'Do not swear at all, either by heaven for it is the throne of God, or by the earth, for it is his footstool, or by Jerusalem for it is the city of the great King.'*

> *'Do not resist an evildoer. But if anyone strikes you on the right cheek, turn the other also ... Love your enemies and pray for those who persecute you.'*

> *'Anyone who divorces his wife except on the ground of unchastity causes her to commit adultery; and whoever marries a divorced woman commits adultery.'*

How does one determine what these sayings mean? They are all introduced by way of contrast with earlier teaching: 'You have heard it said ... but I say to you ...', so all four are offered as a correction, and indeed as more demanding than the teachings they are to replace. But that still leaves their precise meaning unclear. One might, for instance, take the first of them as a rhetorical exaggeration; Jesus did use such figures of speech, as when he said that for a rich man to enter heaven is harder than getting a camel through the eye of a needle. But to do that one has to have made an

---

independent judgement that in one way or another it would be unacceptable to take it literally; and indeed, that Jesus' hearers would have found a literal understanding unacceptable, for the meaning of any statement depends on conventions shared by the speaker and the hearers. But even if some such interpretation is entirely reasonable for the first of these four, it is hard to see how one could take a similar view of the second. Yet Christian tradition quite generally seems to have ignored the second one entirely, without much explanation. Here, as in the case of the third saying about non-resistance to enemies, it seems that the tacit assumption has been that ideals – that one's word is one's bond, and that non-retaliation expresses the forgiveness of God – sometimes have to bow to the pressure of events. Where people's interests are powerfully engaged, one cannot rely simply on their word of honour; additional sanctions, such as divine disapproval, must be brought in as a counter-balance. Similarly with non-resistance. It is indeed an ideal, and can often be practised, but sometimes the cost is just too high. In these last three cases, unlike the first one, we are not dealing with an obvious example of hyperbole, which is never to be taken literally. The view taken on the other three is that the sayings of Jesus *are* meant literally. In the case of the second and third, their force is either that of an ideal, to be observed if possible, or at least that of a principle which is to be observed 'other things being equal'. The difference between these and the first one, then, is a difference of speech–act, and hence of sense, and the justification for distinguishing between them depends upon different judgements about the acceptability of the various ways in which one might interpret them.

But in that case, the interpretation of the fourth one also needs to be justified in the same way as the second and third. If it is to be taken as an absolute prohibition in all circumstances, this reading cannot be justified simply by appeal to the sense of Jesus' saying without any reference to what might be involved in observing it in various situations, as with the discussion of just wars. The fact that Matthew's Gospel includes an exception clause, whereas the version given in Mark and Luke does not,[16] might suggest that Matthew already thought that it might have to be applied differently in

---

[16]   Matt. 5:31–32; Mark 10:3–4, 11–12; Luke 16:18.

different situations. It is also possible that these sayings were all originally intended to be understood as practicable because the Final Judgement was at hand, in a manner similar to Paul's view on avoiding marriage precisely in that context, as already mentioned.[17] In that case, issues arising about how that ideal should be practised given the greatly increased length of marriages might be thought relevant to the problem as it presents itself in our own day.

From this discussion, it is clear that fidelity to Christian moral tradition can be, and has proved to be, very far from the simple notion that fundamentalists might have us believe. As in all cases of translation, so here too, faithful translation is an ideal which can be achieved only with considerable effort to understand all the earlier stages: the Torah which Jesus used as his starting point; the teachings of Jesus himself as they would have been understood by his audience; and also the ways in which that understanding has been translated and retranslated in the practices of different generations. Christian pacifism presents us with a somewhat unusual situation in which contradictory views on an important issue, an issue about the value of life, both flourish in the contemporary Church, which has made no attempt to arbitrate definitively between them. The fundamentalist's simplification of this process is simply unsustainable.

The priestly ordination of women

The question whether to ordain women to the priesthood would be faithful to Christian tradition raises most of these issues in a particularly acute form, since at least at first blush there seems to be almost no room for doubt about what the tradition is. Occasions on which women in the Catholic Church have in fact functioned as priests, if indeed there have been such, have been few and usually confined to small localities over short periods of time. So it is not easy to see how a tradition whose practice has been all but unchanged over centuries could be fairly 'translated' into the opposite of that practice – faithful translation does not in general permit a flat negation of the original! The matter, however, is not quite so straightforward; considering it in some detail will serve to

---

[17]   1 Cor. 7:25–31, see above, p. 128.

illustrate many of the issues we have so far raised about the proper use of authoritative texts and traditions, a use which is faithful to those traditions without being fundamentalist about them.

At least some of the reasons given down the centuries for excluding the ordination of women have relied on arguments which nowadays cannot be sustained. One example of such an argument, found in Aquinas[18] and in several other medieval philosophers, is Aristotle's view that in the animal kingdom quite generally females are defective males, weaker in several ways, and in particular intellectually less strong and over-emotional. Another might be taken from Genesis and is found in Paul and other writers, to the effect that woman was created for the sake of man, and not vice versa; an argument which then gets overlaid with what are plainly culturally conditioned patterns of women's dress and decorum.[19] In the later works in the New Testament there is a concern for conventional decency and order in the Christian household. One can read in Ephesians an endorsement of the ordinary cultural standards of morality, and hence of the customarily accepted roles of men, women, children and slaves in the family and the community more generally.[20] Plainly, these are not views which we would nowadays be willing to endorse, slow though the Christian tradition was to change even its attitude to slavery and women. Considerably later still, in the first letter to Timothy, concern for women's decorum and dress is expanded to include a veto on them teaching in the church, becoming a bishop, or ever being in a position of authority over a man. It is an interesting fact that the writer plainly thought such injunctions necessary, though precise evidence from the relevant period explaining why he should have thought so is lacking, so far as I know. In any event, the claim depends on an interpretation of Genesis 2 which suggests that Adam was sinless compared with Eve, and that his being created first justified a moral precedence.[21] In short, in at least many of the earliest

---

[18]   *Summa Theologiae* I, 92, 1, reply to the first objection.

[19]   1 Cor. 11 3–13. This is perhaps all the more surprising in the light of the scrupulously even-handed treatment of the sexual roles of men and women in 1 Cor. 7. Again, it is almost impossible to reconcile 1 Cor. 14:33–36, in which women are forbidden to speak in church, with Paul's earlier acceptance of women as prophets, and is concerned only with their dress and hair-style. It may perhaps be an interpolation into Paul's text from a later period.

[20]   Eph. 4:25—6:9.

[21]   Eph. 5; 1 Tim. 2:8–15.

Christian churches the pattern of roles gradually shifted from the more radical picture in Paul's letters to one which was more common in secular societies more generally. There is nowadays in the Church no dispute that cultural attitudes towards the role of women in society have themselves changed over the years, although, sadly, those changes are still incomplete and slow-moving. It is therefore accepted that it is a mistake to base claims about fundamental Christian dogmas on such attitudes even if they have persisted for many centuries. Not all aspects even of long-standing traditions are justifiable. More positively, we can perhaps see that the presumption must be against any form of discrimination, unless a good reason can be given for it. The statement of the Biblical Commission, endorsed by Pope Paul VI, makes precisely these points as applied to the ordination of women.[22]

Paul's two earliest letters, written to the Thessalonians, repeatedly address the members of that church as 'brothers and sisters' without distinction. And, as Popes have recently been at pains to point out, Paul makes one of the most forthright statements about non-discrimination when he writes to the Galatians:

> As many of you who have been baptised into Christ have clothed yourselves with Christ. There is no longer Jew or Greek, there is no longer slave or free, there is no longer male or female, for all of you are one in Christ Jesus.[23]

The recent papal documents also insist that women played important roles in many of the early Christian communities. They point out the striking fact that the first witnesses to the risen Jesus mentioned in the Gospels were women, despite the fact that women were not legally recognised as witnesses in Jewish tradition. It is accepted that there were many religious functions which were part of the life of the early Christian communities, such as teaching, prophesying, serving the poor, producing hymns, speaking in tongues, interpreting others when they so speak; and that

---

[22] *Inter Insigniores*, issued in 1976 by the Congregation for the Doctrine of the Faith with the approval of Paul VI, § 4. In 1994 this document was later also endorsed by Pope John Paul II in his letter *Ordinatio Sacerdotalis*. It points out that in several cases like those just mentioned, the various restrictions on the behaviour of women were 'little more than disciplinary practices of minor importance', which have no bearing on how we in our culture ought to behave.

[23] Gal. 3:15, 27–28.

there is no suggestion at all that women could not play their part in all of these.[24] Again, at the end of his letter to the Philippians, Paul bids farewell to three people, the first two of them women, Euodia and Syntyche, then the man to whom the letter was sent, Epaphroditus; Paul describes them all as those 'who have struggled with me in the work of the Gospel together with Clement and the rest of my co-workers'. The two women may be mentioned first because they were the most important, or singled out because they had disagreed with one another. Either way, he seems to be addressing what is in effect a team of equals, though at the beginning of the letter he mentions 'all the saints, and the ministers and overseers'.[25]

None of this is nowadays controversial. On the contrary, the fact that women were so active in the early Christian communities has been used as the basis for what is now held to be the key argument *against* the priestly ordination of women. Since women play such important roles, it is argued, it is clear that the early churches had no general cultural prejudice against them. Surely, then, there must have been a specific objection to their ordination which is not to be explained simply in terms of cultural prejudice. The reason can only be that the early Christians knew that Jesus deliberately did not give women the role of priests. Here is the official statement of that case, as endorsed by Pope Paul VI:

> It has been claimed in particular that the attitude of Jesus and the Apostles is explained by the influence of their milieu and their times. It is said that, if Jesus did not entrust to women and not even to his Mother a ministry assimilating them to the Twelve, this was because historical circumstances did not permit him to do so. No one however has ever proved – and it is clearly impossible to prove – that this attitude is inspired only by social and cultural reasons. As we have seen, an examination of the Gospels shows on the contrary that Jesus broke with the prejudices of his time, by widely contravening the discriminations practiced with regard to women. One therefore cannot maintain that, by not calling women to enter the group of

---

[24] For instance, 1 Cor. 14; Eph. 4:1–16.
[25] Once more there is a problem about translation. The Greek words are *presbyteroi* and *episkopoi*; at this date, however, these words refer to managerial positions, and are certainly not best translated by 'priests' and 'bishops' as they might have been a hundred years later. They are tagged on here in a way that seems a polite way to acknowledge a group of church workers.

the Apostles, Jesus was simply letting himself be guided by reasons of expediency. For all the more reason, social and cultural conditioning did not hold back the Apostles working in the Greek milieu, where the same forms of discrimination did not exist.

The statement does, however, draw an important contrast:

However, the Apostle's forbidding of women to speak in the assemblies (1 Cor 14:34–35; 1 Tim 2:12) is of a different nature, and exegetes define its meaning in this way: Paul in no way opposes the right, which he elsewhere recognises as possessed by women, to prophesy in the assembly (1 Cor 11:15); the prohibition solely concerns the official function of teaching in the Christian assembly. For Saint Paul this prescription is bound up with the divine plan of creation (1 Cor 11:7; Gen 2:18–24): it would be difficult to see in it the expression of a cultural fact. Nor should it be forgotten that we owe to Saint Paul one of the most vigorous texts in the New Testament on the fundamental equality of men and women, as children of God in Christ (Gal 3:28). Therefore there is no reason for accusing him of prejudices against women, when we note the trust he shows towards them and the collaboration that he asks of them in his apostolate.[26]

These arguments are briefly summarised and repeated in John Paul II's letter *Ordinatio Sacerdotalis*, in which he states that this teaching is for those reasons to be held as authoritative:

Wherefore, in order that all doubt may be removed regarding a matter of great importance, a matter which pertains to the Church's divine constitution itself, in virtue of my ministry of confirming the brethren (cf. Lk 22:32) I declare that the Church has no authority whatsoever to confer priestly ordination on women and that this judgment is to be definitively held by all the Church's faithful.[27]

However, since our knowledge of what Jesus intended or did not intend depends on the biblical evidence, it is perhaps possible that

---

[26] *Inter Insigniores*, § 4.
[27] *Ordinatio Sacerdotalis* (1994), § 4.

scholarly inquiry may throw further light on the matter, as has happened on many issues in the past. I make the following tentative suggestions, which incorporate much of what these two papal documents have said, and attempt to take the issue somewhat further.

The key fact to be considered is that Jesus seems to have made remarkably little preparation in any respect for the lives of his followers after his death. It may be that he did not envisage that there would be any great stretch of time for which such prepara-tions might have to be made. The earliest Christian text we have, Paul's first letter to the Thessalonians, is plainly written against the background assumption that the End cannot be long delayed, even though the time is uncertain. Paul consoles the Thessalonians that those who have already died will not be left behind when the End comes, but will join 'those of us still alive'. He encourages his people to console themselves with these words. And very similar assumptions probably underlie what he writes to the Corinthians. [28] Even much later, Mark still seems intent on accepting that the End is near, and Jesus is quoted as saying that all this will happen before the present generation has passed away. Because Mark is writing considerably later, after the destruction of the Temple in AD 70, he wishes to interpret that event as one of the first signs of the imminent wrath to come. So in his Gospel, Jesus predicts the destruction of the Temple, suggests that such an event presages the End, and exhorts the disciples to courage though they know neither the day nor the hour. [29] It is surely likely that the early Christians picked up this sense of imminence and urgency from Jesus himself, and therefore less likely that Jesus handed on to them any longer-term plans for organising a Church.

His choice of the Twelve is explicitly connected to the final restoration of the New Israel, when the Twelve are told that they will rule over the twelve tribes. [30] As the early Christians gradually took on board that the End might well not be imminent, this Jewish symbolism of the final restoration of the twelve tribes became less important. It is therefore not altogether surprising that for the most

---

[28] 1 Thess. 4:13—5:11; 1 Cor. 15:51–58.
[29] Mark 9:1; Mark 13 is entirely devoted to this subject.
[30] Matt. 19:28; Luke 22:30.

part the Twelve disappear from recorded history after the death of Jesus; even their precise names are not entirely clear.[31] The Twelve do appear as a group in Paul's list of those who saw the risen Jesus, but apparently as a different group from 'the apostles'.[32] Peter and John are known because of their position in the Jerusalem church and their dealings with Paul, but the head of the Jerusalem church is James, the brother of the Lord, who was not one of the Twelve. Apart from Peter much later in Rome, there is no evidence of any of the Twelve being a leader in any of the early Christian communities. Rather than the Twelve, it was the leaders of these churches who were normally called 'apostles' and most of the apostles whom we hear about later were not among the original Twelve. We know of several of these apostles by name: Paul, Barnabas, perhaps Sylvanus and Timothy, Junia and Andronicus. To judge by the name, Junia, an apostle in Rome, was a woman, and the Andronicus, described as an apostle in the same breath, might well have been her husband.[33]

So it seems that the early Christian churches developed their own various patterns of organisation, leadership and authority, and that they did not in these respects at least have any specific structures established by Jesus which they felt they had to follow. On the other hand, despite their variety in terms of structure, it is fairly clear that all of them celebrated the Eucharist. The details no doubt varied: the precise words handed down by Paul to his congregation in Corinth and probably used in the liturgy there differ somewhat from another liturgical tradition which we can find in the Gospel of Mark, and again from what we find in Luke and Matthew. I have already argued above that the traditional Jewish remembrance prayer, 'Do this in remembrance of me', does not of itself imply that Jesus was asking *his disciples* to remember him after his death. It was a prayer that his death be an acceptable sacrifice of which *God* would take note. He said that he would not drink wine again until this had been accomplished; and the community in Corinth is required to 'proclaim the death of the Lord until he comes'.

[31] There is a strong but unwritten tradition that Thomas founded a church in India.
[32] 1 Cor. 15:1–9.
[33] Rom. 16:7.

We have little or no evidence of precisely who took part in, or who presided at, the eucharistic liturgy in the earliest communities. What we do know is that towards the end of the first century there were elders and overseers; but beyond the roles that such people would have exercised in synagogues and in families there were no fixed descriptions of how they functioned in a Christian context; and in particular there is no suggestion that they were in any sense sacred or ordained.

All in all, therefore, it seems to me that three conclusions can be drawn concerning the earliest Christian communities:

1   Jesus himself makes no special provision for their organisation: the appointment of the Twelve was a symbol relating to the New Israel in the coming End Time, not an ecclesial act. Jesus shared with the Twelve his authority to interpret the Torah in their preaching of the Kingdom.[34] In the earliest communities there was no expectation of a Church which would last for a long time.

2   The earliest Christian communities plainly had some people who acted as leaders, some of whom were described as 'apostles', only one of whom is known to have been one of the Twelve, and at least one of whom seems to have been a woman. It does not seem in the least likely that they would have regarded any of these people as priests.

3   What the early communities had in common was, as Paul succinctly put it, the belief that Jesus died for our sins, was buried, and was raised on the third day, together with the custom of proclaiming the death of the Lord until he should come, as an act of asking God to remember Jesus' self-sacrifice and associating themselves with it. They 'recognised the body of the Lord', and believed that mysteriously they shared in his life.

4   They took some time to work out their relation to the Jewish Law, to adjust gradually to the realisation that the end might not after all be imminent, and to evaluate the various charisms and manifestations of the Spirit.

---

[34]   'Binding and loosing' refers to giving authoritative interpretations of the Law, not to the forgiveness of sins.

It seems clear, then, that the earliest traditions neither say nor imply anything about the ordination of women, for the very good reason that they say nothing about ordination at all. Jesus did not 'ordain' anyone in our contemporary sense of the term, and we have no evidence of exactly what the status of any of the leaders of the Christian communities was at this time; there is certainly no suggestion that any of them were thought of as 'priests'. We should resist the temptation to attribute to Jesus intentions which are difficult to reconcile with the evidence we have about what he did and what his intentions were in so doing.

Raymond Brown has argued powerfully that, as it gradually became evident that the scattered Christian communities might have an indefinitely long future ahead of them rather than an imminent Second Coming, they needed to develop strategies and structures to ensure their orderly perseverance in the faith and their unity with one another, and that they did so in a variety of ways and at different speeds.[35] These differences of emphasis and style, which we can partly explain from what we know of the location and history of some of these communities, are evident in the later works of the New Testament, the gospel traditions and in the pastoral epistles ascribed to Paul and John.[36] It was only sixty or seventy years or so after the death of Jesus that serious efforts began to be made to have more organised structures, and to establish the collection of writings which were widely accepted as helpful and would eventually come to form our Canon.

The major 'translation', then, of the preaching of Jesus was that undertaken by Paul in explaining the wider significance of Jesus, his life, death, resurrection and teachings. Paul adapted the teachings and religious practices to an audience which included many non-Jews, and incorporated the crucial interpretation of his death and resurrection which we later find in Matthew, and especially in the Gospels of Luke and John. There is no doctrine concerning the priestly ordination of women because there is no doctrine of priestly ordination as such at all. At most there is a tentative view

---

[35] Raymond Brown, *The Churches the Apostles Left Behind* (New York: Paulist Press, 1984). He was one of the two or three best Catholic biblical scholars of the entire century.

[36] They were almost certainly not written by Paul or John themselves; rather they were written in the name of Paul or of John out of the great respect that a later generation had for those apostles.

about feminine decorum, based on an almost incoherent argument on which Paul does not insist. The general experience is that women and men might equally be gifted with the charisms of the Spirit. So if we have anything to learn from the earliest Christians, it would be that the assignment of functions in the community was not determined by considerations of what Jesus did or intended, but depended upon recognition of the presence of the Holy Spirit, through whom the life of the risen Jesus was communicated to his body, the Christian churches. By their fruits you shall know them. We can, and should, translate the practice of later generations of Christians into our own cultures and our own understanding of the various talents which people possess; we should indeed work out how those talents should best be employed in teaching theology, presiding at the liturgy, preaching, and administering the structures of the contemporary Church.[37] We should not assume that there is one office, that of 'priest', which must be held by anyone who has to undertake any of these functions. On all these matters, we surely have much to learn from our history as Church. The notion of a faithful translation presupposes as the only possible starting point a correct understanding of what was said by the statement which we wish to translate, or implied by the practice which we are led by the Spirit to live out in our own ways. In the case of women's ordination, there just is no fixed original statement, and later developments do at least to a great extent reflect the sadly subordinate position of women in many societies down to our own day. We will do best to follow the early churches by trying to discern which are the gifts given to individuals whereby they can contribute to the life of the community in our own times.

What if there is no tradition?

There are many choices we are called upon to make for which at first sight we might expect little or no guidance from tradition, simply because the very possibility of these choices depends upon technologies which simply were not available to our forebears. They could not have imagined the possibilities which might at

---

[37] A stimulating account of what such a church might be like is to be found in Antony F. Campbell SJ, *The Whisper of the Spirit: A Believable God for Today* (Grand Rapids MI and Cambridge UK: Eerdmans, 2008), Part III, 'Belief and God's Phoenix Church'.

some point be available to us, such as organ transplants, or the cloning of humans; or large-scale challenges which confront us as unavoidable, such as those posed by global warming, or population explosion. Does the notion of fidelity to our Christian tradition have anything to say at all about such choices?

There are, of course, general considerations which might bear on such issues, which have nothing specifically to do with Christian tradition at all. On broadly consequentialist grounds we should carry out a risk/benefit assessment, to the extent that we can do such a thing. Sometimes – perhaps with some versions of genetic manipulation – the risks might be so serious and the consequences of failure potentially so terrible that there would be little or no possibility of justifying any course of action in such a case, unless the foreseeable consequences of doing nothing were likely to be at least as bad. Not that it is always easy to decide whether predictions of dire consequences amount to anything more than irrational scare-mongering born of dislike of the unknown, or whether there is the promise of a really important breakthrough. We simply have to do what we can on the basis of the best information available to us, and try not to sweep problems under the carpet because they seem too enormous and too potentially catastrophic to deal with.

But such general considerations are not directly my concern here. I wish to ask whether there are any arguments based upon specifically Christian tradition which need to be considered and their validity assessed. For it is possible to be unjustifiably fundamentalist in trying to approach this question, too, along the lines of 'If God had intended us to fly, he would have given us wings'. As an argument against aeroplanes, that is of course patently absurd, and would not be given serious consideration by anyone. But it is perhaps a form of argument which is not so very different from arguments in other areas which are taken seriously. So it is worth looking rather more closely at the relation of fundamentalism to the Unknown. I shall consider two very different examples as illustrative of many others.

Genetic manipulation

There is nothing wholly new about genetic manipulation. For centuries people have bred animals in order to maximise characteristics thought to be desirable; and in nature species have interbred. There are, of course, limits to what is possible outside the laboratory; but in the laboratory more and more possibilities are opening up. Dazzling prospects are held out to us – the treatment and even cure for genetically influenced illnesses, the elimination of certain malfunctioning genes from the human gene pool, climate- and disease-resistant crops, higher yielding milk-cows; there is even talk of children designed to order, and, perhaps most frightening of all, the distant vision of the creation of beings sufficiently intelligent to perform menial tasks for us, but not sufficiently intelligent to resent having to do so or to suffer from so doing.

Alarm at many of these and other similar proposals is widespread, of course, and I think it takes fundamentally three forms. The first is to emphasise the enormous risks involved in trying to bring many of these promises to fulfilment. It has become clear over the years since the famous discovery of the double helix structure of DNA by Crick and Watson that things are far from being as simple as that model suggests. It is not simply a matter of whether a gene is present or not: genes which are present still may or may not express themselves, or may express themselves in unsuspected ways, depending on complex features of the way in which the strands in the helix are interwoven. At the moment we have extremely inadequate control over the possible outcomes of proposed genetic manipulations and hence over the suffering or the irreversible environmental damage which they might produce. In short, the risk factor is enormous, and the potential benefits may not outweigh those risks.

Other issues relate to risks of a very different kind. The prospect of 'designer children' has what is in principle an acceptable face: for who would not want, were it possible, to have children free of genetic defects which they might in the ordinary course of events have inherited from their parents? The correction or avoidance of acknowledged malfunctions ought not in itself to be controversial. Rather, the problems have to do with the procedures by which such children are produced. But quite apart from those worries, such limited aims often seem like the first step in a process which becomes increasingly unwelcome. Long before one endorsed anything like the aim of producing some kind of Master Race, with its explicit wish to discriminate against or even exterminate other humans, one would still be introducing a distinction between desirable and undesirable characteristics, which would surely lead to serious problems with children who did not possess those features, or who resented the fact that their parents had not wished to try to ensure that they had those features. Besides, the benefits of sheer variety among humans may be difficult to quantify, but they are surely very real for all that.

It might be argued that underlying all these kinds of risk is the religious truth that it is contrary to the divine plan to interfere with the various species that God has created. This view may, but need not, go hand in hand with a denial of evolution on the basis of a misunderstanding of the first chapter of Genesis. For it is possible to believe that the way in which God brought about the existence of species is by having them evolve, while still firmly maintaining that the basic structures of the universe are not for us to interfere with or attempt to manipulate. There are serious risks involved in doing so, as we have discovered, and that fact itself should be taken as confirmation of such policies being a contravention of the will of God. We already know that God saw that the way he had arranged things was good; so it should be no surprise that to initiate any radical modification of that order will result in making things worse in the long run, rather than better.

But there are many problems with this argument. The version of it which denies evolution has to face all the difficulties involved in that denial, and there is no need to repeat those here. But the version which maintains that things have to evolve in the way that God intended them to evolve and in no other can be faced with an uncomfortable dilemma. Taken to extremes, this argument would object to any human attempt to interfere with the workings of the natural world. The harnessing and control of electricity, the development of medicines, the selective breeding of domestic animals and crops, and, for that matter, the erection of buildings and the construction of machinery, are all ways of interfering with the 'natural' course of earthly events. To object to such uses of human intelligence on the grounds that they interfere with nature seems highly dubious even on biblical grounds; for, in creating human beings with such potential abilities, God surely intends these abilities to be used for the benefit of human beings and indeed for the enhancement of the creation entrusted to us. To be sure, there can be objections raised to some human activities – on environmental grounds, for instance; but I cannot see any grounds for a general objection to the use of human skill and invention.

So any argument would have to be based on specific cases rather than general difficulties. In this context it might perhaps be suggested that there is something particularly objectionable in the attempt to manipulate creation at the level of genetic manipulation, even if one grants that there is no general objection on religious grounds to human efforts to use and benefit from the goods of creation. But given the course of evolution, it is difficult to argue that God has any objection to the development of one species of organism from others. That is an entirely natural phenomenon. Moreover, it is common ground among biologists, I believe, that it is in any case almost impossible to give just a single definition of what any given species is. Living creatures differ from one another in many different ways, and one can draw different boundaries between them for different purposes. Hence, exactly at what point the first animal evolved which we ought to consider to have been in the full sense a human being is surely not at all clear. There is a strong argument for saying that we do not have a definition of 'in the full sense a human being' ready-made which could be used to answer that question with any precision. It is nonetheless worth asking ourselves the hypothetical question: how ought we to treat such beings were we ever to be confronted with them? How we should categorise them, and how we ought to treat them, are two ways of putting the same set of issues, raising questions which cannot be settled definitively either by genetics or by appeal to biblical sources more generally. The answer would surely depend upon their needs and on the abilities which we discovered them to have. Exactly in what respects such a being would and would not be like us in relevant ways would be an issue we would have to work out in practice. I conclude that our Christian tradition offers nothing which relates specifically to this question.

Death and life

In contrast to issues concerning genetic manipulation, Christian tradition has had a great deal to say about issues of life and death. We have already seen that two traditions – the older one pacifist, the more recent formulated in terms of legitimate self-defence in general and the just war in particular – have both survived. At least until very recently, Christians quite generally accepted the legitimacy of capital punishment, although that is now more likely to be questioned or even rejected. Interestingly, in the case of legitimate self-defence the shift over the centuries has, if anything, been towards the legitimacy of causing death in carefully specified circumstances, whereas in the case of capital punishment the move has been in the opposite direction, with fewer and fewer types of crime being thought to provide a justification for taking the criminal's life. In both cases, various circumstances have been thought to make a difference to what it is permissible, or even obligatory, to do or not to do. Not since the third century has the right to life been taken to override all other considerations whatsoever.

There are other issues involving life and death which raise issues which are more similar to the ones we have about genetic manipulation, in that additional problems have been caused by developments in technology which earlier Christians simply did not have to consider and about which therefore we have no obviously relevant tradition. One of the more obvious developments has been in the field of intensive care. We have at least the possibility of ameliorating or even curing serious medical conditions which even a few decades ago would have resulted in almost immediate death. One result of this has been that the (somewhat) traditional rule of thumb, 'Thou shalt not kill, but needst not *strive officiously* to keep alive', has more recently proved less than adequate when deciding how much effort and technology one has any kind of duty to employ.[38] The other traditional phrase, much employed by the manuals of moral theology, that nobody is required to use 'extraordinary means' to preserve life, is also a good deal less than clear. Is 'ordinary' to be taken as 'what people would have considered possible in a domestic environment', or 'what, nowadays, would normally be tried in a good hospital' or as 'using widely available technology to its limits'?

In a recent case, an Italian woman, Eluana Englaro, was given nutrition for seventeen years with little if any prospect of recover-

---

[38] Arthur Hugh Clough, 'The Latest Decalogue' (1865). In any case, it was originally intended as an ironic comment on contemporary mores, certainly not as an adequate moral principle!

ing consciousness, though her heart and lungs were functional. In another case, a young man in England, Tony Bland, also with no prospect of regaining consciousness, was maintained on a heart–lung machine for four years. One might well argue that providing nutrition and water are surely very ordinary everyday activities; but it has been held by courts in England that to do so in the circumstances required by either of these two cases would not be routine feeding, but would be a medical treatment (and, by implication, not 'ordinary'). But rather than concentrate on 'ordinary means', British courts have tried instead to focus on the notion of 'being in the patient's best interests' or 'being of benefit to the patient', and have therefore had to try to decide what those best interests might be. In short, the technological possibilities are many, and the moral choices which they now present are both new and complex in ways which earlier generations did not have to face. Our traditions, even to the extent that they are comparatively clear, are inevitably less than adequate guides. In the case of Eluana Englaro, it was asserted by one influential Cardinal that to discontinue that treatment in her case would not simply be allowing the patient to die, but would be an act of homicide. In the case of Tony Bland, the relatives and medical authorities were all agreed, and were eventually allowed by the court to discontinue support.

A couple of paragraphs taken from a long and admirable research paper prepared for the House of Commons will give a good idea of the complexity some of these issues as they would be seen from an informed point of view:

> *The majority in the House of Lords decided that in cases as extreme as Tony Bland's it could be argued that it was not in the patient's best interests to carry on living: that biological life alone, with no consciousness, was not necessarily of benefit to the patient. Thus doctors not only might have no duty to continue providing medical treatment; it could even be argued that they had a duty to stop providing it, since their only justification for treating a patient incapable of consenting was on the grounds that the treatment was believed to be in the patient's best interests. Their Lordships also agreed that artificial nutrition and hydration should be regarded as 'medical treatment' like any other aspect of medical practice, despite arguments from the Official Solicitor that they should be*

regarded as a basic right which no one could be denied.

On the particular issue of the cessation of artificial nutrition and hydration, the guidance restates the view of the House of Lords in Bland that artificial nutrition and hydration constitutes 'medical treatment'. It can therefore be withheld from patients in certain circumstances, in the same way as other forms of medical treatment deemed not to 'benefit' the patient may be withheld, without the courts necessarily regarding the patient as having been 'starved to death' by the doctors involved. The BMA welcomes the categorisation of artificial nutrition and hydration as medical treatment, but states that it recognises that many people do see a big difference between medical treatment and nutrition, regardless of how 'medicalised' the process of feeding the patient may be, and that therefore further safeguards are necessary.[39]

I have two comments to make on such issues.

The first is by way of being a philosophical preliminary. I have pointed out that the borderline between species is by no means as clear-cut as we might once have assumed. It is therefore hardly surprising that the status of our closer ancestors is by no means clear-cut. Were we to be confronted by a Neanderthal would we assume that it must have human rights and be treated as a human being? Or should we say that they had some of those and perhaps not others, not directly as human rights, but in the way in which, controversially enough, we think of chimpanzees as having rights? On what grounds would such a question be settled? For moral purposes, I suggested that instead of a sharp dividing line between species, we ought to think in terms of a spectrum of needs and abilities. One can discuss at what point on this spectrum the notion either of general moral, or of specifically human, rights becomes relevant at all. If we consider the whole range of the attitudes we have to micro-organisms, plants, lower animals, higher animals, humans, it is apparent that we take it that only higher animals and humans can properly be said to have moral rights, and that the criterion is that they are capable of suffering. We have little compunction in killing mice or rats, though we would certainly balk at

---

[39]   Katharine Wright, *Medical Treatment (Prevention of Euthanasia) Bill (Bill 12 of 1999–2000)*, a research summary presented in connection with Mrs Ann Winterton's private member's bill.

causing them needless pain in so doing; even lower animals have a right not to be tortured. Exactly *which* rights higher animals have (to live, to be left undisturbed in their homes, to marry, to be educated, to inherit, to vote, and so on), and at what point they acquire those rights, if they do, and why they do so when they do, is less clear. We can in general say that beings with rights should not be subjected to cruelty and should have their abilities fostered and their needs cared for, of course. But those generalities still leave everything to be played for.

Secondly, in the case of the victims of tragic accidents who are in a persistent vegetative state, or, even more seriously, whose heart and lungs can never again function independently, questions about how they should be treated are often posed in terms of whether switching off life-support machines would be killing them, or simply allowing them to die; or by asking what course of action would be in the patient's best interests. I wonder, though, whether we ought not to ask a much more difficult question: at what point should we say that these persons die? Do they die at the point at which they have once and for all lost the ability to perform those activities which we consider to be fundamental to being a human person, or only at the point at which the last organic function of the bodies has ceased? At what point is it no longer a human life, a human person for which we are caring? Did Tony Bland die shortly after the tragic accident in the football stadium at Hillsborough, or only when his relatives were allowed by the court to discontinue the life-support? If the former is the true answer, then some of the questions which the courts try to answer in such cases – would they be permitting homicide, or merely allowing someone to die, and what would be in the patient's best interest? – would be seen to have already been overtaken by events.

The answer to these questions is, of course, far from obvious. There is at least one good reason why issues about defining species, or what we should regard as a human person, and when a human person has ceased to exist on this earth, are especially difficult. It is that, although these questions have been forced upon us by scientific and technological advances, none of them is strictly speaking a scientific question. This is because there is general agreement about the scientifically discoverable facts. We have a good knowledge of the ways in which the genetics of various organisms are similar and the ways in which they differ; we understand the facts of embryology, neuroscience and trauma, we have a good grasp of the organic requirements for sensation and various degrees of understanding and thought. We can assess brain sizes and neural complexity, and we can roughly assign conscious activities to different sections of the brain in ourselves and in other species. But the disputed questions, questions which often have important moral implications – what constitutes an actual, living human being? Which physical differences should we consider crucial when we come to consider the borderline cases? – these are philosophical questions to which different answers can reasonably be given by people who accept the same empirical facts. The current state of the debate on many of these issues in legal circles, among philosophers and in the view of ordinary people is far from settled. In our legal tradition, in the cut and thrust of philosophical debate, and through the experience of ordinary people, views emerge only gradually over time in the light of decisions taken about particular cases, which can be revisited and perhaps revised. In courts, decisions have to be made; but it is not, I think, normally thought that these decisions are beyond reasonable doubt. The cases have come to court precisely because decent people can produce good arguments for different and incompatible views, where pressures can be very great, and the longer-term implications of policies are often very unclear.

Coping with uncertainty

Especially in the last two sections, but to some extent in this chapter as a whole, we have been dealing with comparatively long-standing problems to which our Christian traditions have not infrequently offered conflicting solutions, as well as with new and unforeseen problems raised by our vastly increasing scientific knowledge and technological abilities, to which no clear solutions seem available. What, then, is left of the notion of fidelity to a tradition in such circumstances? It might be thought that the answer has to be that the notion of fidelity to a tradition simply does not apply. But there is perhaps one more thing that can be said. For I believe that we can find in the history of Christianity a tradition of how best to deal with uncertainty.

A good example of this tradition is to be found in the way in which the Christian Churches in general have dealt with the issues surrounding pacifism and war. The early Christian communities, as we have seen, were in a position where they could interpret the sayings of Jesus on love for enemies and on not resorting to the sword to settle disputes as straightforward prohibitions. Given the closer identification of Christianity with governments, and the need for governments to defend states against enemies, it is clear that many Christians over the centuries came to the conclusion that the interests of large numbers of innocent people justified overriding the prohibition on the use of force and violence, and the reinterpretation of the sayings of Jesus as ideals. Not, note, as *mere* ideals with little or no practical force, for those Christians who defended some version of the just-war theory emphasised that they were bound first to make every effort to make peace. War was a last resort when all else had failed, and had to be pursued in the least damaging manner possible. Nonetheless, the legacy of early Christian pacifism lives on and in our own day inspires dedicated supporters who conscientiously object to being directly engaged in the violence of war. Both views are ardently defended by Christians who are deeply convinced that those who hold the opposite view are utterly mistaken. A similar conflict of views can be seen on a smaller scale with regard to the legitimacy of the death penalty. More generally, comparatively few Christians are consistently 'pro-life' on all issues, if that means holding that it is without any exception wrong to take a human life. Many of those most opposed to abortion, for example, will nevertheless support capital punishment. That the right to life overrides all other considerations has never in practice been a traditional view, despite the frequency with which it is asserted.

The fact is that many Christians are completely committed to their views on any given one of the issues in which the taking of human life is involved, and believe that those who disagree with them on that issue are utterly mistaken. Nevertheless the situation is that on many of these issues incompatible views have traditionally been accepted as legitimate ones for Christians to hold, even if the Church as a whole has at different times been more inclined to one than to the other. This seems to me to be an entirely proper state of affairs in cases where good, but not decisive, arguments can be produced on each side. Conscientious objection to all wars is an obvious case in point. And by 'decisive argument' here I mean one which most open-minded and good people who prayerfully consider the issue in the light of their faith can see has made the opposite view untenable. Where there is no such clarity, it goes against natural justice to insist that people have a religious obligation to believe and follow one side rather than the other. This approach, known as 'Probabilism,'[40] was proposed by the Dominican friar Bartolomé de Molina towards the end of the sixteenth century and subsequently defended also by Jesuits in the seventeenth century. It was bitterly attacked by Pascal and the Jansenists, as also by some orthodox Catholic theologians, on the grounds that it left far too much up to the judgement of individuals, and led in practice to a lowering of moral standards. Of course the test, whether an opinion really can be seriously defended or not, is itself not clear-cut and can be abused. Nevertheless, in one form or another it has long been part of Catholic moral tradition. The basic aim is to try to discover how basic moral principles, or principles derived from the Gospel, should properly be applied in a variety of changing circumstances; and this is done by the discussion of a series of case studies, in exactly the way in which our legal system also tries to make progress.[41] I think it is especially appropriate in the areas we have just discussed, where rapid advances in knowledge and technology make it very unclear how as Christians we should act for the best. There is no better way for us to search for the truth.

What this approach rejects is the kind of specious clarity which fundamentalists wish to rely upon. Their mistake is not in believing that clarity is desirable, nor in trying to derive clear conclusions from their Christian principles. It lies in their reliance on methods of deriving that truth which take it as a given that apparently complex issues are, in the light of Christian faith, not complex at all. As a result, fundamentalists will typically regard their opponents as simply, straightforwardly and obviously unfaithful, rather

---

[40]   From the Latin *probabilis*, meaning 'for which a serious argument can be given'.
[41]   Hence the term 'casuistry' from the Latin *casus*, 'a case'. Like 'Probabilism', 'casuistry' unfortunately came to be a term of abuse, with connotations of dishonest special pleading. But when they are taken with proper seriousness, case studies are the basis of most moral and legal reasoning.

than recognise that in many matters intelligent Christian believers can honestly *and reasonably* hold beliefs with which one disagrees. The result is an intolerance, a too-rapid dogmatism, and often enough a refusal to face facts that is likely in the long run to corrode faith rather than to support it.

To Sum Up

On the analogy of the faithful translation of texts, I have argued that
fidelity to tradition requires three things to be successfully done:

1 The relevant stages in the tradition have to be correctly
   understood.
2 One has to find a way in which to express each of those
   stages in one's own idiom.
3 One has to estimate how one should modify what one says or
   does to take account of factors which some earlier stage(s) in
   the tradition could not have foreseen.

I have argued that fundamentalists underestimate the complexities
of each stage. They assume that it is comparatively easy to understand the earlier stages of one's tradition, and the practices of our
forebears; they assume that it is comparatively easy to translate
texts from previous ages in such a way that they will communicate
effectively to people who live in a world which is very different
from that of the various cultures through which those texts have
already passed. And, what is in some ways most difficult of all, a
judgement has to be made about how, in the light of one's tradition,
one ought to deal with situations, intellectual or practical, which
are now significantly different or perhaps never had previously to
be faced.

   It has proved fatally easy for Christians down the centuries to
assume that they understood their key texts. This complacency was
perhaps encouraged since serious problems arising simply from
the vocabulary and syntax of the earliest Christian texts were
comparatively few, though, of course, they were considerably
more serious in the much more ancient Jewish texts upon which to
varying extents the Christian writers depended. In that very limited
sense the texts were understood, although, as we can now see, with
such examples as Genesis or other parts of the Old Testament and

the Gospels in mind, only very imperfectly. In the late eighteenth and in the nineteenth centuries there was an explosion of knowledge about the history, customs, languages, literature and religions of the ancient world from which those biblical texts – New and Old Testament – originated. Once the history of ancient times became better understood, and we could see what were the political and religious conflicts which confronted the peoples of those regions, it was much easier to situate our traditional texts in their true context. The result is that now the texts can be seen to say things which are often notably different from the ways in which they were traditionally interpreted. Much the same can be said for the way in which the discovery of the Dead Sea Scrolls and the study of other texts, Jewish and Roman, from the period immediately before and contemporaneous with Jesus, have opened a new window on to Jesus' world. We now have a much more nuanced picture of Judaism at that period, and of the Hellenistic world into which the first Christian preachers moved. As a result, our own foundational texts have in a way sprung to life, now that they can be seen in their original context. The other side of this coin, though, is that the task of interpreting them becomes more complex, since there are more possibilities which might have to be considered; and some long-accepted assumptions about the meaning of these texts have been shown to be mistaken. These adjustments are still in the process of being made.

So it is a mistake to think, as many Christians might be inclined to do, about the development of doctrine in too simple a way. It is indeed true that Christian beliefs about Jesus and about their own communities and practices have developed and crystallised; their implications have been more deeply considered over the centuries. But it seems to me that that picture can readily be oversimplified, as though the process of orthodox theology was one of straightforward linear improvement. For two reasons I do not think this is accurate. The first is that it is important to recognise the importance of, and the continuing need for, diversification in Christianity. Christianity has not been an extra dimension in the development of just one civilisation – roughly that of Western Europe. Christianity at its best has tried to translate itself in terms which will speak to cultures which are not Western, and whose members may well each put a different emphasis on, and have a variety of visions of, the ways in which human beings can respond to God, while still sharing a common basic framework because of our shared human nature and our shared Christian origins. The earliest Christian communities were not homogeneous, either in their practices or in their vocabularies, yet they recognised one another as members of the one body of Christ.

✗ The challenges of developing ways of being Christian which genuinely respond to – preach the good news to – the Chinese, the Indians, the Latin Americans, the peoples of Africa, and the unchurched youth of the contemporary 'West' are very real, and cannot be adequately met by insisting on a 'one size fits all' approach; as if one way of putting things, or doing things, communicates equally well with everyone no matter what their own language or customs might be. Secondly, while it is true that Christianity has developed in richness and understanding over the centuries, it has done so to a considerable extent by trial and error. Adequate translations require time to negotiate, unexplored depths of meaning take delicacy to uncover and assess for accuracy. This process needs to be encouraged and fostered, with patience and confidence in the longer-term outcome.[1]

I have already remarked upon the ways in which the imagery of contemporary Christmas cribs is often adapted to include reference to our contemporary cultures, so that cribs in Bolivia, London, Rome and Tokyo will be notably different. To conclude, I offer a very different example of how broadly the same 'message' has been communicated to people in very different cultures. Think of the many ways in which Shakespeare's *Romeo and Juliet* has been interpreted, not merely in the various productions of the professional theatre, but in musicals such as *West Side Story*. Especially interesting for our present purposes, I believe, is a play about the knife gangs of inner London, produced by the Hammersmith Youth Theatre, to whom Latino New York and Renaissance Verona would be equally alien. *West Side Story* is not, of course, a word-for-word translation of Shakespeare; nor is the Hammersmith Youth Thea-

---

[1] The point has, of course, been made in much greater detail by John Henry Newman, *An Essay on the Development of Christian Doctrine*. There is a very helpful recent article on the *Essay* by Gerard H. McCarren, *in* Ian Ker and Terrence Merrigan (eds.), *The Cambridge Companion to Newman* (Cambridge: Cambridge University Press, 2009), pp. 118–36.

tre's production. While it is clearly important to give our contemporaries something of the feel for ancient times, so far as we can, I hope to have shown how limited is the usefulness of word-for-word translations for effective communication across centuries and cultures. Our imagery, language and rituals, if they are to come across to people, including the 'unchurched youth' so often mentioned with a certain desperation, will have to be much more imaginative, though no less faithful to tradition. I am told that at the end of the Youth Theatre play the actors silently threw into the audience a single white rose for each young person who had recently been stabbed to death by local gangs. This rite was the moving climax of an extremely powerful communication process. How often do Christian liturgies communicate as well as that? Sometimes, indeed, they do. Much of the time they do not even begin to.

The antidote to fundamentalism is not to fossilise our beginnings, nor to insulate our preferred features of those beginnings, and then ignore the changing world in which our God has placed us. The need for security which fundamentalism seeks to satisfy is better and more creatively met if we have confidence in the continuing guidance of the Spirit; and the Spirit will be our guide if we faithfully try to use the intelligence and imagination God gave us to translate his word into the many languages of our world.

Index

Adultery 35
Altemyer, Bob 2 n2
Ambrose of Milan 129 n13
Animal Farm 38–9
Antioch, church in 123–5
Apostles
  at Last Supper 88
  early ministry of 113
  later wider use of the term
    136–40
  sources of authoritative truths 63
  witnesses to resurrection 43,
    49–53, 88
Aquinas
  books burned by University of
    Paris 61
  endorsed by Church 60, 61
  just war theory 130
  nature of women 134
  paradoxes of transsubstantiation
    93 n17, 97
Aristotle
  approach contrasted with
    ARCIC on applied to
    Eucharist 96
  re-discovery in the West 60–2
  scientific method contrasted
    with Galileo 64
  used at Trent 91–4, 96,
  view of moral virtues 129 n13
  view on nature of women 134
Austin, J. L. 31–2
Authority
  in fundamentalism generally 36,
    65, 134
  in the Church 60, 68–70, 125,
    126, 137–40
  in Judaism 61, 75, 67
  of Apostles 124

  of God 130
  of Jesus 77, 115
  of scriptures 2–4, 21, 35–6, 65
  of tradition 8, 36
  of women in church 134–5
Averroes 61

Baptist, John the 39–42, 46
Barr, James 1 n1
Barton, John 44, 45
Bellarmine, Cardinal Robert SJ
  62–9
Berengar of Tours 90–4
Brown, Raymond 141

Campbell, Antony F 142 n37
Carroll, Lewis 21 n3
Chalcedon, Council of 76, 81–6
Chenderlin, Fritz 116 n10
China Mission 126–7
Chinese customs 99, 105
Clough, Arthur Hugh 147 n38
Common Law 6,107
Competence, linguistic 22, 24
Conventions, linguistic 21–6, 31,
  33, 45, 65, 66, 71 n10, 99
Crick and Watson 144

Damascus Road, Paul's
  conversion 52
Dawkins, Richard 45
Designer children 144
Didache 89
Divino afflante Spiritu, Pius XII
  70
Double Truth theory 63–4

Endean, Philip 114 n8

Eucharist
  in ARCIC 94–5
  in *Didache* 89–90
  in Fourth Gospel 55, 89
  in Luke 54–5
  in Paul 87–90
  presiding at 140, 142
Evidence
  contrasted with explanation 47,
    56–7
  for resurrection of Jesus 50
  for evolution 68
  for heliocentric theory 72
  for Jesus' intentions 137
  key problem in fundamentalism
    4
  related to culture 57–9
Evolution 4, 67, 68, 71, 145, 147
  compatible with *Genesis*? 145

Factual assertion, recognition of 2,
    38, 45, 46, 56–7, 73
Farley Edward 5, 35
Fitzpatrick, P. J. 93 n17
Fruits of the Spirit 125, 143
Fundmentalism 2
  antidote to 158
  atheist implications of 4–5
  attitude to the unknown 144–6
  conflict with science 41, 62, 64
  first use of term 1
  literal sense of scripture 2, 34,
    36–8, 56
  moral 66, 68
  oversimplification 7, 66, 79, 83,
    116, 126, 134–35, 154–6
  preference for transliteration 86,
    96
  suspicion of missionary activity
    125–6
  rigor about translation 9, 15, 61,
    73, 86
  strategies to defend 3, 38, 42,
    66, 68
Fundamentalists
  defined 4–5
  selective 35–7

Galileo ii, 38—42, 45
  anti-relativist 105
Gandhi 34
Genesis
  interpretation of 37, 68—74,
    134, 145,
  Gillespie, Charles Coulton 67 n7
Gregory of Nazianzen 129

Harris, Harriet A 1 n1
Higher Criticism 2
Hoekema, Dr 34 n3
Human nature 28, 80–4, 110–11,
    149–51
Humani Generis, Pius XII 69
Humpty Dumpty 13
Hunsberger, Bruce 3 n2
Hypostasis, how to translate 75,
    81—7

Ignatius of Loyola 114
Inerrancy of the Bible 68
Intention in actions 100–2
Inter Insigniores, Pope Paul VI
    135 n22
Intercultural dialogue 19, 22, 26,
    29,

Jesus, early beliefs about
  God become man 78
  Lord 81
  Messiah 40, 50, 73, 77–9, 115
  Son of God 39, 46, 77
  truly God 79—87
  Wisdom of God 78

Jesus' family tree 40–41
    'David' as code 42 n6
Jewish Law, observance by
    Christians 123, 140
John XXII, Pope 61

Ker, Ian 157 n1
Kuhn, Thomas 58
Kung, Hans 1 n1

Lamentabili, Holy Office 69 n8
Last Supper 88–90, 97, 114–15
Life on other planets 64
Linear A 20 n2

Maimonides 61
McCarren, Gerard H. 157 n1
Meaning
    conditions for establishing
        17–20
    public rather than personal 22
    scepticism about 21–2
Messianic claims 40, 42, 79, 115,
    125
Metaphor 47, 73, 80
Model Penal Code 100
Modernism 59
    Churches' response to 68–70
Modernists distrusted 1
Moltmann, Jürgen 1 n1
Moral Terms, application of 103–9

Newman, John Henry 157 n1
Noll, Ray R 128 n8
Nicaea, Council of 80, 85–6, 97
Newman, John Henry 98 n108

Ordination
    of women 133, 141–2
Ordinatio Sacerdotalis, Pope John
    Paul II 135 n22
Original Sin 68, 72

Overseers 136

Pacifism 152
Pascendi, Pius X 69
Passove, 76, 88–90, 154
Pentecost 43
Pharisees 41, 98, 119–25
Pluralism, moral 109–12
Post-Modernism
    and meaning 25, 27
    and relativism 24, 26–29

Qur'an
    teaching of 34
    as inspired word of God, 2, 4, 6
Rees, Nigel 18 n1
Relativism 25,104
    about morality 104–6
    contrasted with 'absolutism' 106
    in general 112
    Wittgenstein not relativist 27
Resurrection 39–62, 79, 86 113,
    141
Secularisation 5

Sermon on the Mount 131
Shubin, Daniel H. 130 n14
Sinners, Jesus associating with
    115
Speech acts 31ff
    ambiguity 35–36
    applied to larger units, 46—9
    factual claims 46, 48
    failure to understand 20
    spoken and written texts 19, 33
Steady State Theory 61 n3
Suffering Servant 50

Tax-collectors 119
The Twelve 49, 136, 138–40
Tomb, the empty 51–6
Tradition (see also Authority)

basic agreement about 4
Importance to Chalcedon 75
importance to Nicaea 81
requirements of fidelity 55–65,
    86, 94–7
threat to 62, 69, 70
Translation
    aims of 17–18, 22
    ancient texts 19

basic features of 17–19
Trent, Council of 62, 91–4
Tsohatzidis, S. L. 32 n1

Wittgenstein, Ludwig 27
Wright, Katharine 149
Wright, N.T. 52 n13

Zimbabwe 118